iPHONE 12 U

Your Complete iPhone 12 Manual for Beginners and New iPhone Users with Troubleshooting Tips and Tricks.

Tech Analyst
Copyright @2020

TABLE OF CONTENT

Introduction 16

Chapter 1: Getting Started: 17

    Set Up Your iPhone 17

    Transfer Content to your iPhone from an Android Phone 21

    Turn on iPhone 21

    Turn off iPhone 22

    Going Home on your iPhone 22

    Choose Ringtone on the iPhone 22

    Choose Message Tone 22

    Set/ Change Language 22

    Set/ Change Date andTime 23

    Wake iPhone 23

    Unlock iPhone 23

Chapter 2: Apple ID and iCloud 24

    Create an Apple ID Account 24

    Change Apple ID Password 25

    Sign in to iCloud 26

    Sign Out of iCloud on Your iPhone 26

    Use iCloud Backup 27

    Share a Calendar on iPhone via iCloud 28

    Synchronize using iCloud 28

    Troubleshoot if iCloud isn't Working 29

    Sign in With Apple 29

Save Your Passwords 30

Chapter 3: Use Siri on iPhone 31

Set up Siri on iPhone 31

Activate Siri on the iPhone 32

Add Siri Shortcuts 32

Play Live Radio Through Siri 33

Type to Siri 33

Disable Hey Siri when your Phone is Facing Down 34

Control Voice Feedback for Siri 34

Retrain Siri with your Voice 34

Hide Apps when you Summon Siri 34

Chapter 4: Family Sharing 35

Set Up Family Sharing 35

Add a Family Member 35

Create Apple ID for a Child 36

Modify Group Sharing Settings 36

Disband Family Sharing Group 37

Remove Someone from the Family Group 37

Move a Child to another Family Sharing Group 38

Download Family Members' Purchases 39

Stop Sharing Purchases with Family Members 40

Ask to Buy for Children 40

Share iCloud Storage and Subscriptions with Family Members 41

Set Up Apple Cash Family 41

Share Your Location with Family Members 41

Set up Your iPhone to be found by a Family Member 42

Chapter 5: Use Screen Time 44

Enable Screen Time 44

Set App Limits 45

Set Communication Limits 46

Allow Select Apps at All Times 46

Set Content and Privacy Restrictions 46

Get Report of your Phone Use 47

Chapter 6: The Control Center 48

Access Control Center 48

Modify Access to Control Center From Within Apps 48

Customize Control Center 49

Access Paired Bluetooth Devices from Control Center 49

Connect to Wi-Fi Through the Control Center 50

Chapter 7: Apple Pay 51

Set Up Apple Pay 51

Set up a Default Card 52

Check out with Apple Pay 52

Send Payment in Messages 52

Request Payment 53

Change Card Details 54

Set Up Apple Cash 55

Manage Apple Cash 55

Update Your Contact & Shipping Information 55

Chapter 8: Basic Functions.. 56

Raise to Wake 56

Arrange Home Screen Icons 56

Check Battery Percentage 57

Control Bluetooth.. 57

Update Phone Manually... 57

Control Flight Mode 57

Choose Night Shift Settings 57

Change the Wallpaper.. 59

Use a Live Photo as Wallpaper 60

Customize Haptic Feedback... 60

Lock or Unlock Screen Orientation 60

Screen Brightness... 60

Set up Cellular Service with eSIM 61

Manage Cellular Plans 62

Chapter 9: Dark Mode 63

Enable Dark Mode 63

Automatically Activate Dark Mode 63

Set Your Wallpaper to React to Dark Mode 64

Chapter 10: Notifications... 66

Customize Notification Options 66

Control Notification for Specific Apps 66

Customize Notification Grouping 67

4

Open the Notification Center 68

Manage Notification.. 69

Chapter 11: Location Services...71

Enable Location Services 71

Turn Off Location Services on iPhone Selectively 71

Turn Off Location Services..72

Adjust Location Services Settings for System Services...........................72

Chapter 12: Camera..73

Use Camera 73

Mirror Front Camera...73

Take a Live Photo 74

Take a Photo with a Filter 74

Panorama Mode 74

Take Burst Shots...75

Use Volume Up Button for Burst... 76

Record a Video 76

Video Resolution and Frame Rates 77

Record a Quick Take Video 79

Record a Slow-mo Video 80

Capture a Time-Lapse Video 80

Take a Photo in Portrait Mode.. 80

Align Your Shot.. 82

Preserve Camera Settings 82

Adjust the Shutter Sound Volume 82

Customize View Content Outside the Frame 82

Prioritize Faster Shooting 83

Turn Off Automatic HDR 83

View Your Photos from Camera 83

Read a QR Code 83

Chapter 13: Photos App 84

View Individual Photos 85

Add Captions and View Photo Details 85

Play a Live Photo 85

View Photos in a Burst Shot 86

Play a Video 86

Play and Customize a Slideshow 87

Delete or Hide Photos and Videos 87

Recover or Permanently Delete Photos 87

Edit Your Photos and Videos 88

Mark up a Photo 89

Trim a Video 90

Edit Slow-Mo Videos 90

Edit a Live Photo 91

Add Effects to Live Photos 92

Edit Portrait Images 92

Create an Album 94

Add/ Remove Videos and Photos to an Album 94

Edit an Album 95

Sort Photos in an Album 96

Filter Photos in Albums 96

Organize Albums in Folders 96

Revert an Edited Photo/ Video 96

Send Video Clips in Messages 97

Send Video Clip or Picture in an Email 97

Share and Print Your Photos 97

Apply Filter to a Video 98

Remove Location Details from your Photos 99

Chapter 14: Phone App 101

Answer Call 101

Call a Number 102

Redial or Return a Recent Call 103

Control Call Waiting 103

Control Call Announcement 104

Block Communication from Certain People 105

Manage Your Blocked Contacts 105

Send Unknown Callers to Voicemail 106

Block Spam Callers 106

Make Calls using Wi-Fi 106

Use and Manage Call Forwarding on your iPhone 106

Cancel Call Forwarding on your iPhone 107

Manage Caller ID Settings and Call Logs on your iPhone 107

Clear Call Logs 107

Chapter 15: Contacts App 108

Add Contacts 108

Merge Similar Contacts 108

Copy Contact from Social Media and Email Accounts 108

Add a Recent Caller to your Contact 109

Save the Number you Just Dialed 109

Import Contacts 110

Delete Contacts 110

Add Your Contact Info 110

Create or Edit Your Medical ID 111

Turn on Do Not Disturb 111

Chapter 16: Messages App 112

Set up iMessage 112

Set up Your Device for MMS 112

Compose and Send Message 112

Compose and Send Messages with Pictures/ Videos 113

Reply to a Message 113

Pin or Unpin a Conversation 114

Switch from a Conversation to an Audio Call or FaceTime 115

Create New Contacts from Messages On iPhone 115

Mute Conversations 116

Share Your Name and Photo 116

Specify View for your Profile Picture and Name 117

Customize Your Memoji and Animoji 118

8

Send and Share Your Location 118

Delete a Message or Conversation 119

Mention People in a Conversation 120

See Mentions in Messages 120

Change Group Name and Photo 120

Send Money with Apple Pay in Messages 121

Request a Payment 122

Manage Notifications for Messages 122

Assign a Different Ringtone to a Contact 122

Chapter 17: Mail App 123

Set up Mail Account 123

Add Additional Mail Accounts 123

Customize Your Email Signature 124

Choose a Default Email Account 124

Delete Email Account 124

Compose and Send Email 125

Reply to an Email 126

Quote Some Text When Replying to an Email 126

Always BCC Yourself 126

Send Email from Different Accounts 127

Block Spam and Unknown Senders 127

Block a Contact Through Their Emails 128

Unblock a Sender 129

Block a Contact Via Settings App 129

Unblock a Contact 129

Receive Notification of Replies 130

Mute Email Notifications 130

Reorder Your Mailboxes 130

Delete Emails 131

Recover Deleted Emails 131

Archive Instead of Delete 131

Decide How Long To Keep Deleted Emails 132

Print an Email 132

Chapter 18: Manage Applications and Data 133

Install Apps from the App Store 133

Delete Apps 133

Share or Give an App 133

Use an App Clip 134

Remove App Clips 135

Move Between Apps 135

Switch Between Open Apps 135

Force Close Apps in the iPhone 135

Multitask with Picture-in-Picture 136

Delete Apps Without Losing App Data 136

Control Automatic App Update 136

Modify Settings for Background App Refresh 137

Configure Your iPhone For Manual Syncing 138

Move Apps around the Home Screen 139

Return the Home Screen to its Original Format 140

Explore the App Library 140

Add New Apps to Home Screen and App Library 141

Perform Quick Actions 141

Chapter 19: The Reminders App 143

Create a Reminder 143

Add SubTasks 144

Create a List 145

Add a List to a Group 146

Today Notification Feature 147

Use Siri as a Reminder 147

Mark Reminder as Complete 148

Edit Multiple Reminders 148

Edit a Reminder 148

Share a List Using iCloud 148

Chapter 20: Find My 149

Set Up Location Sharing 149

Share Your Location 149

Stop Sharing Your Location 149

Respond to a Location Sharing Request 150

Stop Receiving Location Sharing Request 150

Add an iPhone, iPod Touch, or iPad 150

Find Missing Device 151

Get Direction to a Device 152

11

Remove a Device from Find My 152

Disable Activation Lock 152

Chapter 21: Apple Maps 153

Use Your Precise Location on Maps 153

View Details about a Place 153

Share Places in Maps 153

Use the Look Around Feature in Apple Maps 154

Explore New Places with Guides 155

Choose Your Preferred Type of Travel 156

Get Driving Directions 156

Get Cycling Directions from Your Current Location 157

Turn Off Voice Directions 158

Chapter 22: Safari 159

Access Website Settings for Safari 159

Access Safari Download Manager 159

Auto-Close Open Tabs in Safari 160

Modify Where Downloaded Files from Safari are Saved 161

Choose When Downloaded File List is Cleared 162

Enable Content Blockers in Safari 163

Temporarily Disable Content Blockers in Safari 163

Block Pop-Ups 164

Share or Save a Safari Web Page as a PDF 164

Translate a Webpage 165

Open Link in New Tab 165

Bookmark a Webpage 165

Add Webpage to Favorites 165

Add Website Icon to your Home Screen 166

Browse Open Tabs 166

Chapter 23: Gaming 167

Pair your iPhone with an Xbox One controller 167

Pair your iPhone with a DualShock 4 167

Unpair Game Controller from your iPhone 168

Chapter 24: Screenshots 169

Take a Screenshot 169

Scan a Document 170

Sign a Document 171

Create a Screen Recording 171

Chapter 25: Wifi and Connectivity 172

Join a Wi-fi Network 172

Control Wi-fi Setup 172

Control Mobile Data 172

Control Automatic Use of Mobile Data 172

Control Data Roaming 172

Use Your iPhone as a Hotspot 173

Download Large Apps over Cellular Network 173

Chapter 26: Battery Tips 175

Set Optimized Battery Charging 175

Disable Auto Update of Apps 176

Stop Background Apps Refresh 176

Extend the Device Battery Life 177

Reduce Screen Brightness 177

Disable Auto App Suggestions 177

Stop Motion and Animations 178

Disable Wi-Fi When Not in Use 178

Disable Bluetooth 179

Locate the Battery Draining Apps 179

Ensure that Personal Hotspot is Disabled 179

Disable Location Services 179

Disable Cellular Data 180

Disable Data Push 180

Set Emails to Download on Schedule 181

Set up the Screen to Auto-Lock Sooner 181

Disable Fitness Tracking 182

Disable AirDrop When Not in Use 182

Disable Automatic Upload of Photos to iCloud 183

Stop Sending Diagnostic Data to Developers or Apple 183

Disable Vibrations 183

Other Helpful Tips to Improve the Longevity of Your iPhone Battery 184

Chapter 27: Troubleshooting the iPhone 12 185

Restart/ Soft Reset iPhone 185

Hard Reset/ Force Restart an iPhone 186

Factory Reset your iPhone (Master Reset)..186

Back-Up iPhone Using iCloud..187

Back-Up Using Mac..187

Back-Up Using Windows PC..188

Restore iCloud Backup 188

Restore a Computer Backup 188

Chapter 28: Conclusion 189

Introduction

The iPhone 12 is Apple's mainstream flagship phone for 2020. The phone comes in a 6.1-inch size and includes Apple's latest A14 chip, improved camera, OLED display, and faster 5G cellular network.

Apple introduced the iPhone 12 alongside the iPhone 12 mini, iPhone 12 Pro, and iPhone 12 Pro Max on October 13. This iPhone model is perfect for anyone that does not fancy the Pro camera features.

iPhone 12 offers users 5G connectivity for improved gaming, better quality video streaming, higher definition FaceTime calls, and faster downloads & uploads.

The iPhone 12 lineup is the first device to have the A14 Bionic chip, which brings efficiency and speed improvement. The A14 Bionic chip offers 40% more transistors than the A13 Bionic chip for faster performance and better battery life. Apple confirms that the A14 Bionic chip is 50% faster than the chips found in other top smartphones on the market in 2020.

iPhone 12 has a battery life of 2,815mAh and offers up to 11 hours of streaming video playback, 17 hours of video playback, and 65 hours of audio playback.

The device is equipped with 4GB RAM and a dual-lens camera that differentiates it from the iPhone 12 Pro models. Apple included a lens correction feature to correct any distortion caused by the super wide-angle lens.

Chapter 1: Getting Started:

Set Up Your iPhone

Setting up your device is the first and most crucial step to getting started with your iPhone. Follow these steps for a seamless experience.

1. Firstly, you need to power on your device. To do this, press and hold the side button – you will see **"Hello"** in various languages.
2. Swipe up on your screen to begin set up.
3. A prompt will come up to select your language and country/region. Choose the correct details.

4. Next is to manually set up your iPhone by tapping **"Set up Manually."** You can use the **"Quick Start"** option if you own another Apple device on iOS 11 or later – place the two devices close to each other, then follow the onscreen instruction. Proceed with the manual setup if you do not have any other iOS devices.

5. You have to connect your phone to a cellular or Wi-Fi network to activate your device and continue with the setup. You should have inserted the SIM card before turning on the phone if going with the cellular network option. To connect to a Wi-Fi network, tap the name of your Wi-Fi network. If there is a security lock on the Wi-Fi, the screen will prompt you for the password.

6. Next is to set up your Face ID. The face ID feature allows you to authorize purchases and unlock your devices. To set up face ID, tap **Continue** and follow the instructions on the screen. You can push this to a later time by selecting **"Set Up Later in Settings."**

7. The next prompt is to create a six-digit passcode to safeguard your data. Tap **"Passcode Option"** to set up a four-digit passcode, custom passcode, or even no passcode.

8. If you have an existing iTunes or iCloud backup, or even an Android device, you can restore the backed-up data to your new phone or move data from the old phone to the new iPhone. Choose the applicable option on the **Apps and Data** screen, then follow the prompt to complete.

In the absence of no backup or if this is your first device, select **"Don't Transfer Apps & Data."**

9. To continue, you will need to enter your Apple ID. If you have an existing Apple account, enter the ID and password to sign in. If you don't have a current Apple ID or have forgotten the login details, select "**Forgot Password or Don't have an Apple ID?**"

10. Turn on automatic updates and set up other features.
11. Set up Siri or tap **Set Up Later in Settings** to skip.
12. Set up Screen Time or tap **Set Up Later in Settings** to skip. Screen time will let you know the amount of time you spend on your device.
13. Click on "**Get Started**" to complete the process. And now, you can explore and enjoy your device.

Transfer Content to your iPhone from an Android Phone

You can move contents to your device from an Android device when setting up your phone for the first time or after a factory reset. To do this, follow the steps above until you get to the **Apps and Data** screen.

- Connect the Android device to an active Wi-Fi.
- Download and install the **"Move to iOS"** app on the android. Then launch the app.

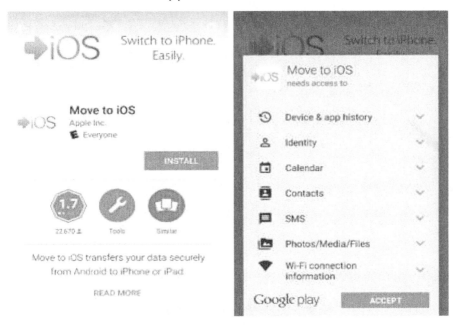

- Go to your iPhone 12, under **Apps and Data,** click on "**Move Data from Android."** Click on **Continue** on the two phones.
- Then follow the instructions you see on the screen to move data from the Android to the iPhone.

Turn on iPhone

- Press the **Side** button until the iPhone comes on.

- Once you see the Apple logo, release the button and allow your iPhone to reboot for about 30 seconds.

Turn off iPhone

- Hold any of the volume buttons and the side button at the same time. Release the buttons once you see the power off slider.
- Move the slider to the right to turn off the phone.

Going Home on your iPhone

- From any screen, swipe your phone screen from the bottom up to return to the home screen.

Choose Ringtone on the iPhone

- From the Home screen or App Libray, go to **Settings**.
- Click on **Sounds & Haptics.** Then click on **Ringtone.**
- You may click on each of the ringtones until you find the one that you want. Select the one you want to finish.
- Swipe the page from the bottom up to return Home.

Choose Message Tone

- From the Home screen or App Libray, go to **Settings**.
- Click on **Sounds & Haptics.** Then click on **"Text Tone."**
- You may click on each of the message tones until you find the one that you want. Then select the one you like.

Set/ Change Language

- From the Home screen or App Libray, go to **Settings**.
- Click on **General**. Then click on **Language and Region**.

- Click on **iPhone Language** to give you options of available languages.
- Choose your language from the drop-down list and tap **Done**.
- A pop-up will appear on your screen, prompting you to confirm your action. Click on **Change to (Selected) Language**.

Set/ Change Date andTime

- From the Home screen or App Libray, go to **Settings**.
- Click on **General**. Then click on **Date & Time**.
- Turn on **Set Automatically** to allow the iPhone to set the time and date using the time zone you are in.
- Turn on **24-Hour Time** to display the hours from 0 to 23.

Wake iPhone

Three ways to wake your iPhone

- Tap the screen, raise the phone, or press the side button.
- Press the side button to put the iPhone to sleep.

Unlock iPhone

- Raise the phone or tap the screen to wake it, then stare into the phone to unlock it with Face ID.
- Swipe up from the bottom of the screen to go home.

Chapter 2: Apple ID and iCloud

Create an Apple ID Account

Your Apple ID is the account that you use to access iOS services like Apple Music, FaceTime, iCloud, iMessage, and more. You can use a single Apple ID and password to sign in to all your Apple services.

- Open the **Settings** app.
- At the top of your screen, click on **Sign in to your iPhone**.

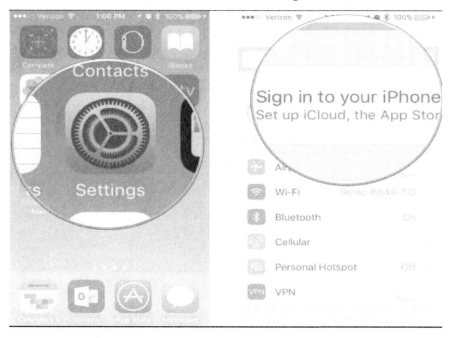

- Choose **Forgot Password or Don't have an Apple ID?**
- A pop-up will appear on the screen; click on **Create Apple ID**.
- Input your date of birth and click on **Next**.
- Then input your first name and last name, then click on **Next**.
- The next screen will present you with the email address option. Click on **"Use Your Current Email Address"** if you want to use an

existing email or click on **"Get a Free iCloud Email Address"** if you want to create a new email.

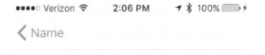

- If using an existing email address, input your email address and password.
- If creating a new one, select the option, and type your preferred email and password. Verify the new password.
- The next option is to select 3 Security Questions from the list and provide answers.
- Agree to the device's Terms and conditions to proceed.
- Select either **Merge** or **Don't Merge** to sync the data saved on iCloud from reminders, Safari, calendars, and contacts.
- Click **OK** to confirm that **"Find My is turned on."**

Change Apple ID Password

- Go to Settings, tap your name, then select the option to change your password.

Sign in to iCloud

iCloud is a cloud computing and storage service from Apple. You can save your photos, contacts, videos, documents, backups, etc. on the iCloud and access it anytime using your Apple ID. All Apple users get free 5GB storage. You will need to purchase more storage space once you exhaust the free space.

- Go to the **Settings app.**
- At the top of your screen, click on **Sign in to your iPhone**.

- Enter your Apple ID email address and password.
- Tap **iCloud** and then toggle on the iCloud features you want to use.

Sign Out of iCloud on Your iPhone

- From the **Settings app,** click on **your name.**
- Click on **Sign Out** at the bottom of the screen.

- Input your Apple ID password, then select **Turn Off.**
- Chose the data you will like to keep a copy of on your iPhone
- At the top right corner of your screen, click on **Sign Out.**
- Click on **Sign Out** again to confirm your decision.

Use iCloud Backup

To use the iCloud backup, ensure that your device is connected to Wi-Fi before you begin. You also need to connect your phone to a charging point while the process is on. To back up, follow the steps below

- Go to **Settings,** click on your name, then tap **iCloud.**
- Toggle on **iCloud Backup.** Then click on **Back Up Now.**
- On this same screen, you will find the date and time of the last backup.

Share a Calendar on iPhone via iCloud

To share your calendar, it is essential to turn on the iCloud for calendar option. Kindly follow the steps below:

- On your iPhone, go to **Settings.**
- Click on your device name at the top of the screen, and select **iCloud.** Then turn on **Calendars.**

After you must have done this, you can now share your calendar by following these steps:

- Open the **Calendar** app on your device.
- At the bottom of your screen, select **Calendars.**
- You will see an ⓘ icon next to the calendar you want to share; click on the icon.
- Select the **Add Person** option on the screen, then pick the people you wish to share the calendar with.
- Tap **Add,** followed by **Done** at the top of your screen.

Synchronize using iCloud

To synchronize your phone details on iCloud, follow the steps below:

- Click on your na,e in the **Settings** app.
- Click on **iCloud.**
- Scroll down to **iCloud Drive** and move the switch left or right to enable or disable.
- Under **iCloud,** click on **Photos.**
- Scroll down to **Upload to My Photo Stream** and slide left or right to activate or disable.

Troubleshoot if iCloud isn't Working

If your iCloud isn't working, follow the steps below to troubleshoot:

- Ensure that Wi-Fi is connected and reliable as this is usually the main reason for iCloud backup not responding.
- Once done, confirm that you have sufficient space in the cloud. Apple gives you only 5G free. If you have used up the free space, clear the files you don't need or back them up with iTunes, then remove them from the iCloud backup.
- If you do not wish to delete any information, the next step will be to purchase an additional room on iCloud.
- Finally, remove any irrelevant data from the iPhone before you perform the iCloud backup.

Sign in With Apple

Not so many of us are comfortable using their Instagram login details to sign in to several apps. This feature allows you to sign in to apps without inputting your personal information.

- Click on the **"Sign in with Apple"** option on a participating website or app. Sign in with Apple will automatically fill in details from your Apple ID.
- Select **Share My Email** or **Hide My Email.** If you choose not to share your email, Apple gives you a random email address linked to your Apple iCloud email address. Any email sent to this random address will be automatically forwarded to your registered email address.

- Tap **Continue** and authenticate with your device passcode or Face ID.
- When next you want to sign in to that website or app, simply tap **Sign in with Apple,** then authenticate with your Face ID or passcode.

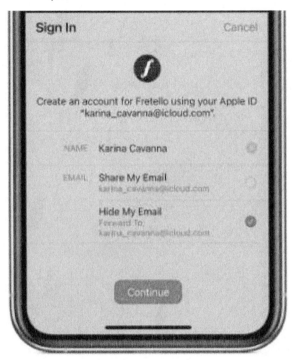

Save Your Passwords

Each time you log in to an app or service, you will receive a prompt to save your password to the iCloud keychain. You can also manage your details manually with the steps below.

- Go to the settings app and click on **Passwords & Accounts**.
- Then click on **Website & App Passwords** and authenticate with your passcode or Face ID.

Chapter 3: Use Siri on iPhone

Apple's virtual assistant is a delight to work with, everyone loves Siri, and most of the time you spend with her involves getting an answer, but she can do more than answer questions.

Set up Siri on iPhone

To use Siri on your iPhone, you have to set it up like you set up Face ID.

- Click on **Siri & Search** from the **Settings** app.
- Toggle on the switch beside **Press Side Button for Siri**.
- A pop-up notification will appear on the screen; select **Enable Siri**.
- Toggle on the switch beside **"Listen to Hey Siri"** and follow the instructions you see on your screen.

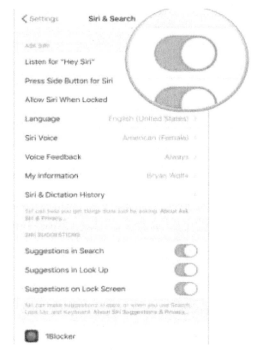

- To use Siri when your phone is locked, activate the **"Allow Siri When Locked"** option.
- Click on **Language** and select the desired language.
- Go back to the previous screen.
- To change Siri's voice, click on **Siri Voice** and choose a voice.
- Go back to the previous screen.
- Click on **Voice Feedback** and choose your preferred option.
- Go back to the previous screen.
- Navigate to **"Search and Siri Suggestions"** and move the slider to the left/ right to turn on or off.
- Now Siri is set up and ready to be used.

Activate Siri on the iPhone

There are two ways to activate Siri on your iPhone.

- **Voice option.** If you enabled "Hey Siri," you can begin by saying "Hey Siri" and then ask Siri any question.
- The second option is to use the side button. To wake Siri, hold the side button, and ask your questions. Once you release the side button, Siri stops listening.

Add Siri Shortcuts

Siri now has an app that makes it easier and faster to assign functions to the virtual assistant.

- Click on the **Shortcut app** to launch it.

- Then click on **Create Shortcuts** to create a simple type of shortcut.
- With the **automation** tab, your device can intelligently react to context as they change. For instance, you can customize the shortcut to play a particular song each time you get home or design the button to automatically send your location to your partner once you leave the office at the end of the day.
- In the **Gallery** tab, you will find a range of predefined shortcuts to give you some inspiration in designing yours, or you can even make use of the predefined shortcuts.

Play Live Radio Through Siri

Siri has access to over 100,000 radio stations from different parts of the world. You can ask Siri to play live radio stations by saying, "Hey Siri, "play [name of radio station] radio station." So long as Siri can access the requested radio station, you will hear the station play instantly.

Type to Siri

You can type your request to Siri instead of speaking. To turn on the feature,
- Go to Settings and click on **Accessibility.**
- Tap **Siri,** then toggle on **Type to Siri.**
- To make a request or ask a question, first summon Siri, then enter your question or task in the text space on your screen.

Disable Hey Siri when your Phone is Facing Down

Place your phone face down to prevent Siri from listening to your voice summon.

- Tap **Accessibility** in the Settings app.
- Select **Siri,** then turn off **Always Listen for "Hey Siri."**

Control Voice Feedback for Siri

Configure how and when you want Siri to give verbal responses.

- Tap **Accessibility** in the Settings app.
- Tap **Siri,** then choose an option on your screen: **Only Speak with Hey Siri, Don't Speak in Silent Mode,** or **Always Speak Responses.**

Retrain Siri with your Voice

When you set up Siri for the first time, you will see a prompt to train Siri to know your voice. You can retrain Siri if it finds it difficult to recognize your voice.

- Tap **Siri & Search** in the Settings app.
- Disable **Listen for "Hey Siri,"** then turn it on again.

Hide Apps when you Summon Siri

Hide active apps each time you summon Siri.

- Tap **Accessibility** in the Settings app.
- Select **Siri,** then disable **Show Apps Behind Siri.**

Chapter 4: Family Sharing

Family sharing permits members of a family group to share purchases, subscriptions, screen time information, iCloud storage plan, and more without sharing their accounts. One person creates the group and then adds other family members. The group owner sets the features or items that can be shared in the group.

Set Up Family Sharing

- Tap your name in the Settings app.
- Select **Family Sharing,** and use the instruction on your screen to create a group. Add up to five people to the group or create an account for your child.
- Choose the features or items that group members can share.

Add a Family Member

Only the group owner can add people to the group.

- Tap your name in the Settings app.
- Select **Family Sharing,** tap **Add Member,** then tap **Invite People.**

- Continue with the instructions on your screen to complete.

Create Apple ID for a Child

The group owner can assign a group member as a Parent or Guardian for a child in the group. Then the group owner or the guardian can create Apple ID for the child. To create Apple ID for a child,

- Tap your name in the Settings app, then tap **Family Sharing.**
- For the guardian or parent, tap **Add Child,** then proceed with the onscreen instructions.
- For the group owner, click **Add Member,** tap **Create an Account for a Child,** then proceed with the onscreen instructions.

Modify Group Sharing Settings

Change the group's sharing setting with the steps below

- Tap your name in the Settings app, then tap **Family Sharing.**

- Tap a new feature to set it up, then continue with the onscreen instructions.
- Click on an existing feature to modify it.

Disband Family Sharing Group

Only the group owner can disband the family sharing group.
- Tap your name in the Settings app, then tap **Family Sharing**.
- Tap your name again, tap **Stop Using Family Sharing** to leave the group, or tap **Stop Using Family** to disband the group.

Remove Someone from the Family Group

To remove someone from your group, the person has to be at least 13 years and above. Members below 13 years can only be transferred to a different group.
- Tap your name in the Settings app, then tap **Family Sharing**.
- Select the person and then tap **Remove (Member) From Family**.

Move a Child to another Family Sharing Group

Children under 13 years need an invitation from another group owner to move to a new group. To invite a child to your group,

- Tap your name in the Settings app, then tap **Family Sharing.**
- Select **Add Family Member,** click **Invite in Person,** and then continue with the onscreen instructions.
- Ask the other group owner to accept the invitation to move the child.

Download Family Members' Purchases

Group members, maximum of 6, can share Apple Books, Apple TV, iTunes, and App Store purchases. All items are billed to the Apple ID account of the group organizer/ owner.

To download shared purchases from the iTunes store,

- Go to the iTunes Store, tap **More,** and then select **Purchased.**
- Choose a family member and click on a category.
- Click the purchased item and tap ⬇ to download.

To download purchases from Apple Books

- Go to the Apple Books app and click your profile picture or the ⓘ icon at the top right.
- Tap a family member under **Family Purchases,** then select a category.

- Tap **Recent Purchases, Genre,** or **All,** then tap ☁︎ beside the purchased item to download.

To download shared purchases from the app store,

- Go to App Store and click 👤 or your profile picture.
- Select **Purchased,** tap the family member, and then tap ☁︎ beside the purchased item to download.

To download from Apple TV,

- Open the Apple TV app, tap **Library,** tap **Family Sharing,** and choose a family member.
- Click on a genre or category, tap the purchased content, and then tap ☁︎ to download.

Stop Sharing Purchases with Family Members

Adult and teen family members can choose to disable purchase sharing for themselves.

- Tap your name in the Settings app, then tap **Family Sharing.**
- Tap **Purchase Sharing** and then turn off **Share Purchases with Family.**
- The group owner can tap **Stop Purchase Sharing** to stop sharing purchases for all group members.

Ask to Buy for Children

The group owner, guardian, or parent can require children in the family group to request approval for their purchases and free downloads.

- Tap your name in the Settings app, then tap **Family Sharing.**
- Tap **Ask to Buy,** select a child, and then turn on **Ask to Buy.**
- If there is no child in the group, tap **Create a Child Account** or **Add Child,** then proceed with the onscreen instructions.

Share iCloud Storage and Subscriptions with Family Members

Group members can share subscriptions and iCloud storage with each other.

- Tap your name in the Settings app, then tap **Family Sharing.**
- Click on a subscription and proceed with the onscreen instructions.

Set Up Apple Cash Family

The group owner can set up an Apple Cash account for a child, then monitor transactions on the Wallet app, view card balance, and choose the people that the child can send money to.

- Tap your name in the Settings app, then tap **Family Sharing.**
- Tap **Apple Cash,** select a child, and tap **Set up Apple Cash,**
- Then proceed with the onscreen instructions.

Share Your Location with Family Members

The group owner's location is shared automatically if they turn on Location Sharing when setting up the group. Other group members may share their location if they desire. When you share your location, the group members can see your location at any time and can help to locate your missing device. To use this feature, you need to turn on Location services,

- Tap **Privacy** in the Settings app, then turn on **Location Services.**

You can now proceed with sharing your location with the group:
- Tap your name in the Settings app, then tap **Family Sharing.**
- Click **Location Sharing,** and then turn on **Share My Location.**
- Select **Use this iPhone as my Location** if displayed.
- Select the family members you want, and then tap **Share My Location.**
- To stop sharing your location with a member, click on the family member, and then select **Stop Sharing my Location.**

To send your location to your family members,
- Open a conversation in the Messages app, then tap the family member's name or profile picture.
- Tap and then select **Share My Location** or **Send My Current Location.**

Set up Your iPhone to be found by a Family Member

For your family member to help find your missing device, you need to do the following:
- Turn on **Find My iPhone:** go to Settings, tap your name, click **Find My,** select **Find My iPhone,** then toggle on **Find My Network, Find My iPhone** and **Send Last Location.**
- Share your location with family members: Tap your name in the Settings app, tap **Family Sharing,** click **Location Sharing,** and then turn on **Share My Location.**

If all these settings are on, follow the steps below to locate a missing device:

- Go to Find My and tap **Devices**.
- Click on the missing device to see its location on the map. iPhone will return with a "No Location Found" message if the system cannot locate the missing device.

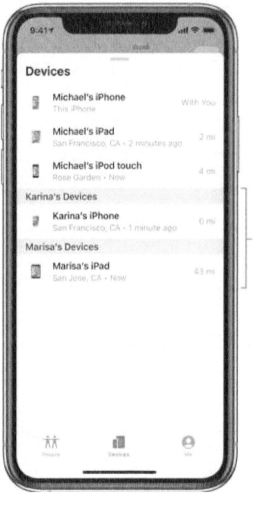

Family members' devices appear below yours.

Chapter 5: Use Screen Time

This feature helps you monitor how much time you spend on your device – you will see the complete details showing the hours you spent on your iPhone.

Enable Screen Time

- Tap **Screen Time** in the **Settings** app.
- Click on **Turn on Screen Time** to enable the feature.

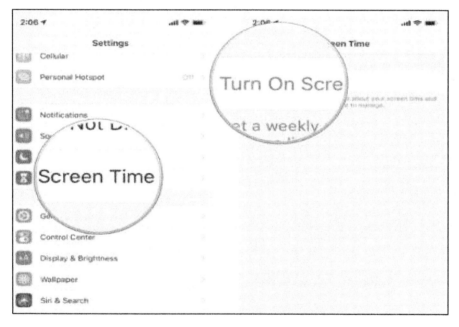

- Press **Continue,** then press **This is my iPhone.**
- Tap **Downtime,** and then enable **Downtime.**
- Choose either **Customize Days** or **Every Day,** then create the start and end times.

Set App Limits

Use the **App Limit** feature of the Screen Time to set the length of time you want to spend on certain apps. Follow the steps below to guide you.

- Tap **Screen Time** in the **Settings** app.
- Select **App Limits,** then click on **Add Limit.**

- Select the app categories and tap **Next.** To create a limit for individual apps, click on the category name, then select an app.
- Choose the amount of time for the App Limit. To set different times for different days, tap **Customize Days,** and set a limit for selected days.
- Tap **Choose Apps** to create app limits for more apps or categories.
- Tap **Done** to save.

Set Communication Limits

Block outgoing and incoming communications like phone calls and messages from select contacts, either at all times or within a period.

First, turn on Contacts in iCloud

- Tap your name in the Settings app, tap **iCloud,** turn on **Contacts.**

Then,

- Tap **Screen Time** in the **Settings** app & tap **Communication Limits.**
- To limit communication at any time, select **During Screen Time,** and then choose the people the limit applies to.
- Choose **During Downtime** if you want the communication limit to work during downtime alone. You may then choose who the limit should apply to.
- Once the communication limit is active, you won't receive communication from the affected people, nor will you reach them.

Allow Select Apps at All Times

Choose apps that should always work regardless of limits or downtime.

- Tap **Screen Time** in the **Settings** app, then click **Always Allowed.**
- Tap ⊖ or ⊕ to remove or add apps from the **Allowed App** list.

Set Content and Privacy Restrictions

Set restrictions for iTunes and App Store purchases as well as block offensive content.

46

- Tap **Screen Time** in the **Settings** app, and then click on **Content & Privacy Restrictions.**
- Turn on **Content & Privacy Restrictions,** then tap **Options** to create content allowances for content rating, iTunes store purchases, app use, etc.
- To prevent modifications to the maximum headphone volume, select **Reduce Loud Sounds** and choose **Don't Allow.**

Get Report of your Phone Use

See how to get a report on your device usage.

- Tap **Screen Time** in the **Settings** app, then click **See All Activity.**
- Click on **Day** to view a summary of your daily use or **Week** for a weekly report.

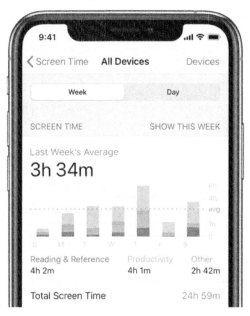

Chapter 6: The Control Center

Control center gives you instant access to things you use most on your phone like taking pictures, controlling your Apple TV, and lots more.

Access Control Center

- Swipe down from the right top side of your screen.
- Click on a function to either open it or enable/disable.
- Move your finger up the function to modify its settings.
- Swipe up to exit the control center.

Modify Access to Control Center From Within Apps

You may choose to access the control center when using other apps. Here is how to enable or disable this option:

- Tap **Control Center** in the Settings app.
- Beside the **"Access Within Apps"** option, move the switch to the right or left to turn it on or off.

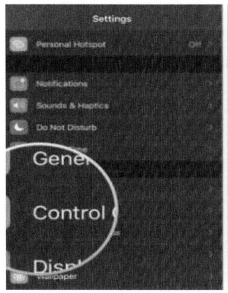

Customize Control Center

- Tap **Control Center** in the Settings app.
- Click on **Customize Controls.**
- Click on ⊖ sign beside the functions you want to remove, then tap **Remove** to delete.
- To add icons to the control center, scroll to **More Controls,** and click on ⊕ by the left side of an icon.
- To reorder the icons, click on the ≡ icon beside each function and drag the function to the position that you want.
- And you are done.

Access Paired Bluetooth Devices from Control Center

You can easily access paired devices on your iPhone without having to exit a particular app. If you need to pair a device to Bluetooth, follow the steps below from any screen:

- Open the control center and tap 🚫 to turn on **Bluetooth,** then click on a Bluetooth device to connect to it.

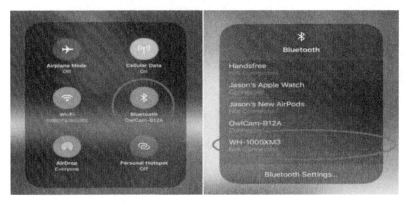

Connect to Wi-Fi Through the Control Center

Here is a faster and direct way to connect to Wi-Fi that does not require launching the settings app.

- Open the Control Center and tap 📶 to turn Wi-Fi on.
- The next screen will display all nearby Wi-Fi networks that have been paired previously regardless of their connection status.
- Tap one to connect.

- The next screen will display all nearby Wi-Fi networks that have been paired previously regardless of their connection status.
- Choose your preferred one to connect.

Chapter 7: Apple Pay

Apple Pay allows you to make secure and contactless purchases on the web, in-store, and on your iPhone. The service also allows you to receive and send money to your family and friends right from the Message app.

Set Up Apple Pay

- You need to add your card, either debit, credit, or prepaid cards to the Wallet app on your iPhone.
- Ensure that you are signed in to iCloud using your Apple ID.
- Using Apple Pay on more than one device will require you to add your card to each of the devices.

Follow the steps below to add your card to Apple Pay:

- Open the Wallet app and click on ⊕. Enter your Apple ID if prompted.
- Enter your card details manually or scan using the iPhone camera – you can add as much as 12 cards. You may be asked to add cards linked to your iTunes, cards you have active on other devices, as well as cards that you removed recently. Choose the cards that fall into the requested categories and enter the security code for each card.
- Tap **Next,** and the information you inputted will go through your bank or card issuer for verification and confirmation.
- Once the card is verified successfully, click **Next** to begin using Apple Pay.

Set up a Default Card

The first card you add to the Wallet app will serve as your default card. To change,

- Touch and hold a different card, then drag it to the front of the stack.

Check out with Apple Pay

After shopping and you need to make your payments at a checkout terminal, the steps below would guide you on check out using Apple Pay:

- Double-press the side button to open the **Apple Pay** screen. If you want to pay with a card that is not your default, tap the default card and choose a separate card.
- Look at the iPhone screen to verify the attempt with Face ID (or enter your passcode).
- Then place the iPhone near the payment terminal.
- If you're using Apple Pay Cash, double-press the side button to approve the payment.

Send Payment in Messages

- Go to Message and tap an iMessage conversation.
- Tap and enter an amount.
- Click **Pay,** enter a comment if you like, and then tap .
- Review the payment information, and then authenticate your transaction.

- After you send the payment, you cannot cancel once the receiver accepts the payment. Tap the payment bubble and then click on **Cancel Payment** to cancel the payment if applicable.

Note: if you do not see the Pay button, tap the button first, then tap the Pay button.

Request Payment

Ask others to send you payment.

- Open an iMessage conversation with the sender, tap Pay and specify an amount.

- Click on **Request,** and then send your payment request.

Change Card Details

View your card details, remove a card or update card details.

- Open Wallet, click on a card, then tap 〰.
- Click on the entry under **Billing Address** to change the billing address for the card.
- Click **Transaction** to view your recent history. Turn off **Transaction History** to hide this information.
- Tap **Card Number** to view the last four digits of the card number.
- Tap **Remove this Card** to delete the card from Wallet.

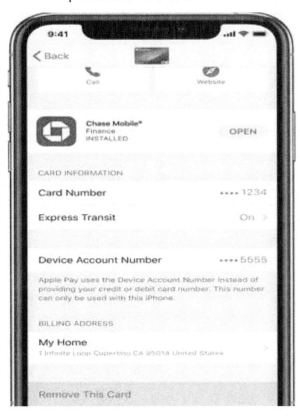

Set Up Apple Cash

Any money you receive in the Message app is added to your Apple Cash card – you can then send it to your bank or spend right from the Apple cash balance.

When someone sends you money via the Message app, the money is added to your Apple Cash card. You can then spend the money from the Apple cash balance or send it to your bank account.

- Tap **Wallet & Apple Pay** in the Settings app.
- Then turn on **Apple Cash.**

Manage Apple Cash

- Tap the Apple Cash card in the Wallet app.
- Your recent transactions will show at the top of the screen. Scroll down to view all your transactions grouped by year.
- Tap ••• and then select an option on the next page – transfer money, request a statement, update your bank account information, and so on.

Update Your Contact & Shipping Information

Follow the steps below to update your contact and shipping details.

- Tap **Wallet & Apple Pay** in the Settings app.
- Then select an option on your screen to update it: Email, phone, or shipping address.

Chapter 8: Basic Functions

Raise to Wake

Wake your phone by raising the device. To turn it on,

- From **Settings,** go to **Display & Brightness.**
- On the next screen, besides **Raise to Wake,** move the slider left or right to enable or disable.

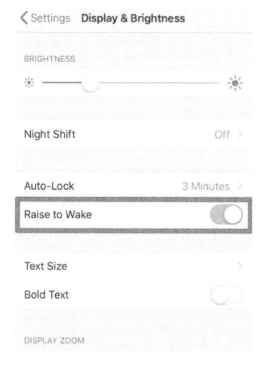

Arrange Home Screen Icons

Follow the steps below to arrange the icons on your home screen:

- Press and hold any icon until all the icons begin to wiggle.
- Drag the icons into your desired position.
- Tap either the **Done** button at the upper right side of the screen or swipe up to exit the wiggle mode.

Check Battery Percentage

- Swipe down from the top-right corner to view the battery percentage.

Control Bluetooth

- From **Settings,** click on **Bluetooth.**
- Toggle on the Bluetooth switch, then click on a Bluetooth device on the list to pair.

Update Phone Manually

- From **Settings,** go to **General** and click on **Software Update.**
- If there is a new update, it will show on the next screen.
- Click on the update to install it

Update Phone Automatically

Turn on **Automatic Updates,** and your phone will update whenever there is a new update.

- From **Settings,** go to **General** and click on **Software Update.**
- Tap **Customize Automatic Updates,** then choose to download and install new updates automatically.

Control Flight Mode

- From the top right side of the screen, slide downwards.
- Tap the airplane icon to enable or disable flight mode.

Choose Night Shift Settings

Night Shift automatically turns your screen colors to a warmer color to make the display easier on your eyes.

- From the **Settings** app, click on **Display & Brightness**.
- Click on **Night Shift** at the bottom of your screen.

- Toggle on the switch beside **Scheduled,** then follow the instruction on the screen to select a duration for the Night Shift.
- To enable Night Shift immediately, toggle on the button beside **Manually Enable Until Tomorrow.**
- Below the **Color Temperature** option, pull the slider to the left or right until you get your desired color temperature.

Change the Wallpaper

- Tap **Wallpaper** in the Settings app and select **Choose a New Wallpaper.**
- Choose a photo from your album or choose an image from Live, Stills, or Dynamic. Wallpapers marked with ⊙ adjusts appearance when you turn on Dark Mode.
- Drag to adjust the image to your liking, and tap **Set.**
- Then choose an option from the pop-up:
    - Set Home Screen
    - Set Lock Screen
    - Both

Use a Live Photo as Wallpaper

Use a Live Photo as wallpaper on the lock screen.

- Tap **Wallpaper** in the Settings app and select **Choose a New Wallpaper.**
- Tap **Live** and then select a Live Photo. Or, click your Live Photos album and then choose a Live Photo.
- Tap **Set,** then select either **Set Lock Screen** or **Set Both.**

Customize Haptic Feedback

System Haptics is responsible for the vibrations you hear or feel when you have incoming calls and alerts.

- Tap **Sounds & Haptics** in the Settings app, then turn **System Haptics** on or off.

Lock or Unlock Screen Orientation

Lock the screen orientation to prevent it from changing when you rotate your iPhone.

- Open the Control Center and tap 🔓 to lock or unlock. When locked, you will find the 🔒 icon in the status bar.

Screen Brightness

Adjust your bright brightness manually or automatically.

- Tap **Display & Brightness** in the Settings app, then pull the slider to adjust the brightness manually.

- To adjust screen brightness automatically using your iPhone's current light conditions, tap **Accessibility** in the Settings app, select **Display & Text Size,** and then enable **Auto-Brightness.**

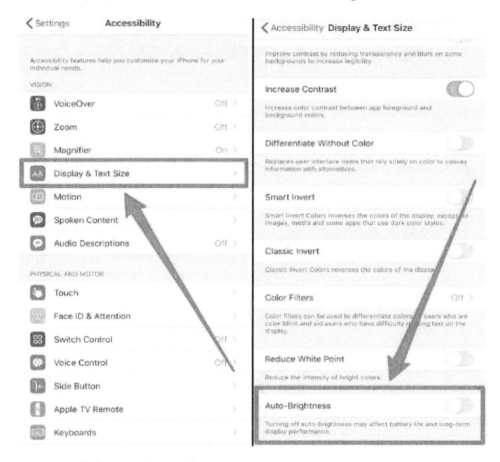

Set up Cellular Service with eSIM

Apart from the physical SIM, you can also install an eSIM on your iPhone. These types of SIMs are stored digitally on the iPhone. To set it up,

- Tap **Cellular** in the Settings app, then tap **Add Cellular Plan.**
- Use your phone camera to capture the QR code provided by your carrier or enter the details manually.

- Then tap **Add Cellular Plan** and proceed with the onscreen instruction.

You can have more than one eSIMs on your iPhone, but you can only use one eSIM per time. To switch between eSIMs,

- Tap **Cellular** in the Settings app, choose a plan, and tap **Turn on This Line.**

Manage Cellular Plans

If you have a dual SIM iPhone, you can customize how you want to use each SIM.

- Tap **Cellular** in the Settings app, click **Cellular Data** and choose a line for your cellular data. The **Allow Cellular Data Switching** option allows the iPhone to use any available line for data. Enable the option if you like.
- Tap **Default Voice Line** and select a default line for making voice calls.
- Choose a line under **Cellular Plans,** then modify settings like Wi-Fi calling, SIM Pin, Cellular Plan Label, or Calls on Other Devices.

Turn on Wi-Fi calling to receive calls on one line when the other is occupied.

Chapter 9: Dark Mode

Your phone's brightness may be blinding due to the bright white theme, especially when you pick up the iPhone in the early hours of the morning. Dark mode helps moderate the brightness of your phone.

Enable Dark Mode

The steps below will show you enable the Dark Mode.

- Go to the Settings app. Click on **Display and Brightness**
- On the next screen, you will see options for **Light** and **Dark** under Appearance. Tap on any of the options you want to activate

Automatically Activate Dark Mode

You do not always need to go to the settings each time you need to activate the dark mode theme. You can set up your phone to automatically change to the bright theme in the day and the dark theme at night with the simple steps below:

- From the settings app, click on **Display and Brightness.**
- Scroll and toggle on the switch next to **Automatic.**

- By default, the menu will change to **Sunset to Sunrise**.
- If you want to change this selection, click on **Options** under the **Automatic** menu.
- **Sunset to Sunrise** uses your GPS location to activate the Dark mode feature once the sun goes down.
- You can select *Custom Schedule* and input your own desired time for the Dark Mode to kick in.

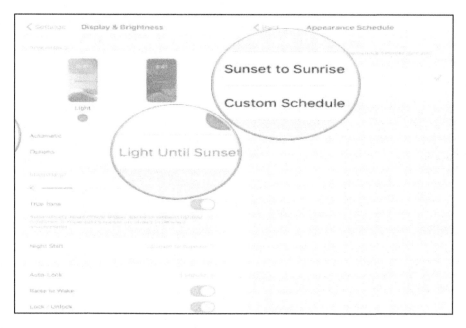

Set Your Wallpaper to React to Dark Mode

Wallpapers on your iPhone can react when your phone is on Dark Mode. The first step is to select a wallpaper that has a dynamic color-changing feature.

- From the settings app, click on **Wallpapers**.

- Select *Choose a New Wallpaper*, click on **Stills,** and select a wallpaper.
- Every wallpaper that reacts to Dark Mode has the ◉ icon under each wallpaper.
- Each image has two sides, with the second side giving a display of how the wallpaper will look in Dark mode.

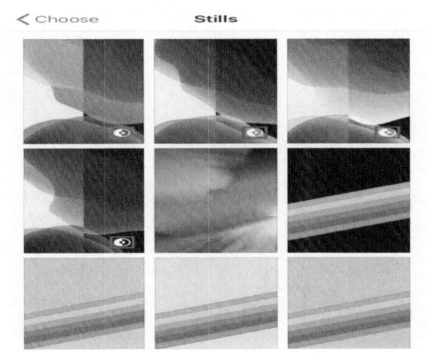

Chapter 10: Notifications

Customize Notification Options

- From Settings, go to **Notifications.**

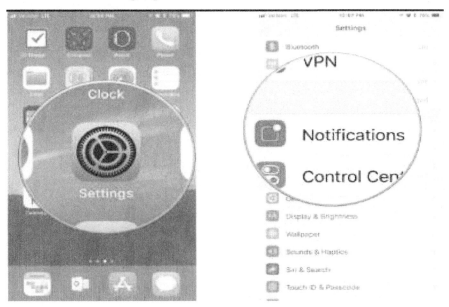

- To choose when you want notification previews to show, click **Show Preview** & then select **When Unlocked, Never,** or **Always.**
- To set this to only when the device is not locked, click on the option **"When Unlocked."**
- To disable notification preview, select **"Never."**
- Click on the Back arrow at the top left of the screen.

Control Notification for Specific Apps

To choose notification settings for individual apps, follow below:

- From Settings, go to **Notifications.** Click on a specific application.
- Toggle on **Allow Notifications** to allow notification for that app.

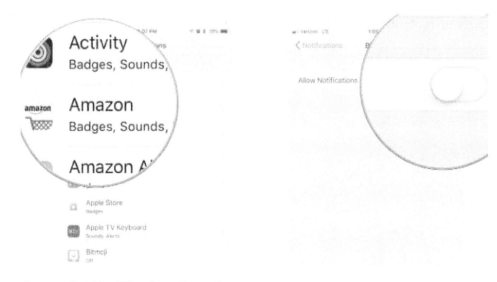

Customize Notification Grouping

Group notifications by categories or apps.

- From Settings, go to **Notifications.**
- Click on the apps that you want to customize group notification.

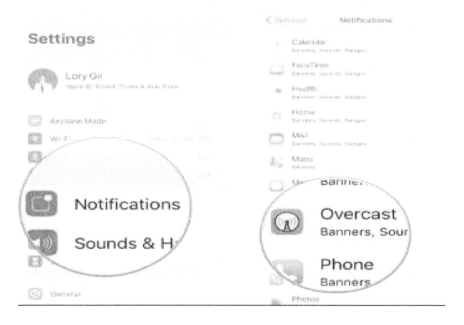

- Scroll down the page and click on **Notification Grouping.**
- Choose your preference from the displayed option:
    - ✓ **Automatic:** Notifications from the selected app will be grouped based on criteria within the app, e.g., thread.
    - ✓ **By App**: group together all notifications from an app.
    - ✓ **Off** to disable notification grouping.

Open the Notification Center

Notifications are saved in the Notification Center if you do not read them immediately they show. To view your notifications in the notification center,

- Swipe down from the top center of your screen or swipe up from the middle of the lock screen. Scroll through the notifications.

- Click on a group of notification to expand it. Tap **Show Less** to close the group.
- Press and hold a notification to view it and perform quick actions on compatible apps.
- Click on a notification to launch the app that has the notification.
- To remove all the notifications in the Notification Center, tap ⊗ and then select **Clear.**
- Swipe up from the bottom of your screen to close the Notification Center.

Manage Notification

To manage your notifications from the Notification Center or lock screen,

- Swipe left over a notification or group of notifications.
- Tap **Manage,** then tap **Deliver Quietly** to turn off sounds for incoming notifications from the selected app and show the notifications only in the Notification Center.
- Tap **Turn Off** to disable notification for that app.

Chapter 11: Location Services

Location services use Bluetooth, GPS, cell tower locations, and crowd-sourced Wi-Fi hotspots to determine the iPhone's approximate location.

Enable Location Services

- Tap **Privacy** in the Settings app, then turn on **Location Services.**

- Toggle on all the apps that should have access to your location data.
- Once selected, chose the option **While Using the App.**

Turn Off Location Services on iPhone Selectively

Turn off location services for select apps that you do not want to access your location data.

- Tap **Privacy** in the Settings app, then click on **Location Services.**
- You will see all the apps that can and cannot access your location. For the apps you wish to access your location information, find such apps, click on them, and select **While Using the App.** For apps that should not access your location details, click on them, and choose **Never.**

Turn Off Location Services

- Tap **Privacy** in the Settings app, then turn off **Location Services.**

Adjust Location Services Settings for System Services

System services like location-based ads and location-based suggestions use Location Services. To view or change the settings,

- Tap **Privacy** in the Settings app, then click on **Location Services.**
- Tap **System Services** to view the status for each service or disable Location services for each service.

Chapter 12: Camera

Use Camera

- From the Home screen, tap the Camera app .
- Swipe left or right to get to **Photo** mode.
- Tap 🔄 or 🔄 to switch to the front camera for a selfie.
- Click the flash icon ⚡ at the top of the screen to enable, if desired.
- To set a timer, tap ⌃ and then click ⏱.
- Set the camera lens to point at the object you want to capture
- Draw two fingers apart/ together on the screen to zoom in or out
- Click on the shutter icon ⭕ or any of the volume buttons to take a picture.

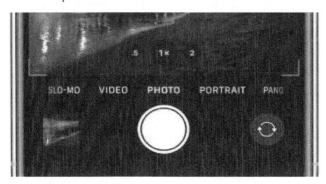

Mirror Front Camera

Let your selfie photos appear as if you are staring into the mirror. To set this up,

- Tap **Camera** in the Settings app, then turn on **Mirror Front Camera.**

Take a Live Photo

A Live Photo records the scene just before and after taking a picture, including the sounds in the environment. To take a Live Photo,

- Swipe to Photo mode and tap ◎ to turn on Live Photos.
- Tap the Shutter button to take your picture.

Take a Photo with a Filter

Add filters to your photos.

- Swipe to Portrait or Photo mode and tap the ⌃ button.
- Tap ◉ to display the filters, swipe through the filters, and then click on one to use it.

Panorama Mode

Panorama mode is perfect for shooting landscapes and other views that won't fit on your camera screen.

- Swipe to Pano mode and tap the Shutter button.
- Slowly pan in the direction of the arrow while keeping it on the centerline. Rotate your Phone to landscape orientation to pan vertically or tap the arrow to pan in the opposite direction.
- Tap the shutter button again to stop.

Take Burst Shots

Burst mode gives you several high-speed photos. You can use either the front or rear camera with this mode.

- Swipe the shutter button to the left and hold to capture Burst shots.
- Lift your finger to stop.
- Tap the Burst thumbnail at the bottom of your screen to view all the photos. Tap **Select** to choose the photos you want to keep. Tap all the photos you want to save, then tap **Done.**
- Tap 🗑 at the bottom of the screen to delete the entire Burst.

Use Volume Up Button for Burst

Touch and hold the Volume up key to take Burst Shots.

- Tap **Camera** in the Settings app, then turn on **Use Volume up for Burst.**

Record a Video

- Swipe left or right to get to **Video** mode.

- Set the camera lens to point at the object you want to capture.
- Click on the **Record** icon, which is the round icon at the bottom of the screen.
- Draw two fingers apart/ together on the screen to zoom in or out
- Press any of the volume keys or tap the Record button at the bottom of the screen to stop recording.

Video Resolution and Frame Rates

By default, video recording is at 30 fps (frames per second. But you can change the frame rate and the video resolution.

- Tap **Camera** in the Settings app and select **Record Video.**
- Customize each option as you want. The higher the resolution and the faster the frame rate, the larger the video file.

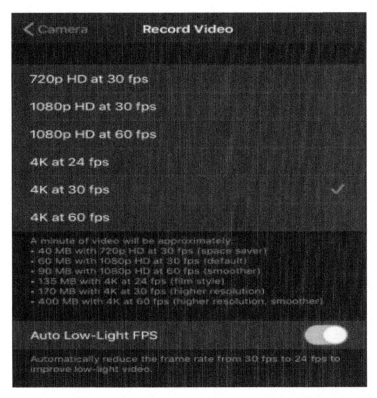

You can also use the quick toggles in the camera viewfinder to change the frame rate and video resolution.

- Switch to Video mode, then tap the quick toggles in the upper-right side of your screen to screen between 4K or HD recording, as well as choose a frame rate.

 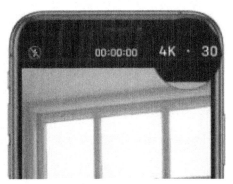

Record a Quick Take Video

QuickTake videos are videos you record in the Photo mode.

- Swipe to Photo mode, then press and hold the shutter button or any of the volume buttons to begin shooting your video.
- To lock the recording and go hands-free, slide the shutter button to the right until it locks with the second image in the bottom right.
- Press the Shutter button to take a photo while recording.
- Tap the Record button to finish.

Record a Slow-mo Video

When you shoot a Slow-mo video, your video records as usual – you only see the slow-motion effect during playback. You can then edit the slow-motion action to have different start and end times.

- Swipe to Slow-mo mode, tap 🔄 to switch to the front camera if you want.
- Press any of the volume keys or tap the Record button at the bottom of the screen to start or stop recording.

To change the slow-motion resolution and frame rate,

- Tap **Camera** in the Settings app and select **Record Slo-mo**.
- Then customize each option as you want.

Capture a Time-Lapse Video

Record footages at different intervals to make a time-lapse video of an experience over a period – like traffic flowing.

- Swipe to **Time-Lapse** mode and position your iPhone to capture the scene in motion.
- Choose between 1× and 2× to zoom in or 0.5× to zoom out.
- Press the Record button to start or stop recording.

Take a Photo in Portrait Mode

Portrait mode adds studio-quality lighting effects to your photos.

- Swipe to **Portrait** mode and use the onscreen tips to frame your subject in the yellow portrait box.

80

- Drag the ⬚ button to select a lighting effect:
    - **Natural Light:** the subject is in sharp focus, and the background blurred.
    - **Contour Light:** the face is decorated with dramatic shadows.
    - **Studio Light:** gives the photo an overall clean look.
    - **Stage Light:** gives a deep black background.
    - **High-Key Light Mono:** gives a white background with a grayscale subject.
    - **Stage Light Mono:** just like Stage Light, but with a black and white background.

- Use the slider under each effect to adjust the intensity of the lighting effect.

- To adjust the background blur, tap ⓕ and then use the slider to adjust the effect.

- You can also adjust the intensity and position of each Portrait lighting effect to sharpen the eyes or smooth and brighten facial features. Tap the ⬢ button at the top, then use the slider to adjust the effect. Press the Shutter button to take a shot.

Align Your Shot

Display a grid on your screen to help you straighten your shots.

- Tap **Camera** in the Settings app, then turn on **Grid**.

Preserve Camera Settings

Preserve the last filter, depth, camera mode, Live Photo, and depth settings you used so that they are available the next time you launch Camera.

- Tap **Camera** in the Settings app and tap **Preserve Settings**.
- Then Turn on all the desired features on the next screen.

Adjust the Shutter Sound Volume

- Use the volume buttons to control the volume of the shutter sound.

Customize View Content Outside the Frame

The camera preview shows scenes outside the camera frame to help you see what can be captured by using a different lens in the camera system. To disable this feature,

- Tap **Camera** in the Settings app & disable **View Outside the Frame**.

Prioritize Faster Shooting

This setting ensures that images are processed faster when you tap the Shutter button. The setting is turned on by default. To disable,

- Tap **Camera** in the Settings app & disable **Prioritize Faster Shooting.**

Turn Off Automatic HDR

The HDR setting of the Camera app helps you to take great shots in high-contrast situations. The camera shoots several photos in quick succession and different exposures and then blends all the images to add more shadow and highlight detail in the photos. The iPhone automatically turns on this feature whenever it's most effective. To disable automatic HDR,

- Tap **Camera** in the Settings app & disable **Smart HDR.**

You can now manually turn on HDR when you like.

- Open Camera and tap **HDR** at the top to turn it on or off.

View Your Photos from Camera

After you capture a photo,

- Tap the thumbnail image on the bottom left side of your screen.
- Swipe through the recent photos and tap ⬆ to share a photo.
- Tap the screen to show the controls.
- Tap **All Photos** to see all your photos and videos.

Read a QR Code

To use the Camera app to read a QR code

- Open Camera and use the camera lens to capture the QR code.
- Click the notification on your screen to open the app or website.

Chapter 13: Photos App

The Photos app ✻ organizes your photos and videos by days, months, years, and all photos. At the bottom of the Photos app, you will find four tabs:

- **Library**: organizes videos & photos by days, months, & years.

Tap to share, play movie, and see location on a map.

Tap to view full screen.

- **For You:** a personalized feed that displays your featured photos, shared albums, memories, and more.

84

- **Albums:** for the albums you shared or created and your photos broken into different album categories.
- **Search:** to quickly search for photos by its caption, date, objects they contain, and location.

View Individual Photos

To see all your photos at once, click the Libray tab, then tap **Months, Years, Days,** or **All Photos.**

- Click on a photo to open it in full screen.
- Double-tap or pinch closed or pinch out to zoom out or zoom in.
- Tap ♡ to favorite a photo or ⬆ to share the photo.
- Tap the back ‹ button or drag the photo down to return to all photos.

Add Captions and View Photo Details

You can search for videos and photos by caption when you use the Search tab.

- Open a video or photo, then swipe up to write a caption in the text field under the image.
- You will also see the location the photo was taken and people identified in your photo.

Play a Live Photo

A Live Photo ◉ records the scene just before and after taking a picture.

- Tap a Live Photo to open it, then press and hold it to play.

View Photos in a Burst Shot

You will find all images of a Burst Shot in a single photo thumbnail. Open the thumbnail to view all the photos and choose the ones you want to save separately.

- Tap **Select** when you open the Burst Shot thumbnail.
- Click on all the photos you want to save, then tap **Done**.
- Select **keep Everything** to retain the Burst and the selected photos or select **Keep Only (Number) Favorites** to discard the photos you did not select.

Play a Video

You will notice that the videos in the Library tab auto-plays as you scroll. Click on a video to play it in full screen, then do any of the below:

- Tap the screen to show the player controls under the video, then use the player controls to mute, unmute, pause and play. To hide the controls, tap your screen.
- Tap your screen two times to move between fit-to-screen and full screen.

Play and Customize a Slideshow

A slideshow collects your photos, formats them, and set to music.

- Go to the Library tab, choose either **All Photos** or **Days,** then tap **Select.**
- Select the photos you want to add to the slideshow, then tap the ⬆ button.
- Choose **Slideshow** from the displayed options, tap the screen, and select **Options** in the bottom right to change the music, theme, etc.

Delete or Hide Photos and Videos

- Open a video or photo, then tap the 🗑 button to delete.
- To hide it, tap the ⬆ button, then tap **Hide.**
- Deleted content stays in the **Recently Deleted** album for 30 days before they are permanently removed from the device.
- Hidden photos stay in the Hidden album.

Recover or Permanently Delete Photos

To recover the photos you deleted or to delete them permanently,

- Go to the Albums tab, scroll to **Other Albums** and choose **Recently Deleted.**
- Tap **Select** and choose the items you want to recover or delete, then scroll down and tap **Delete** or **Recover.**

Edit Your Photos and Videos

- Open a video or photo in full screen, then tap **Edit.**
- To crop the image, tap ⌗ , then drag the corners to choose the area of the photo you want to keep. Tap ▇ to crop the image to a standard preset ratio, tap ⟲ to rotate the photo 90 degrees, or tap ◁▷ to flip the image horizontally.
- To adjust the color or light, swipe left under the picture to see the editing buttons for each effect like Brilliance, Highlights, etc. tap a button, then use the slider to adjust the effect. Tap the effect button to see the photo before and after you applied the effect — tap 🪄 to automatically edit your videos or photos with effects.
- Tap 🎨 to apply filter on the image or video – click on a filter, then use the slider to adjust the effect. Tap the photo to compare the edited image to the original.
- Tap **Done** to accept the changes or tap **Cancel** and then select **Discard Changes** to return to the original photo.

Mark up a Photo

To annotate a photo,

- Open the photo and tap **Edit.**
- Tap the ••• button, then tap **Markup** Ⓐ.
- Use the different drawing tools and colors to annotate the photo.
- Tap ⊕ to add your signature, add a shape or text.

Trim a Video

Adjust the length of a video.

- Open a video and tap **Edit.**
- Drag the left end of the frame viewer to choose a start point, then drag the right end of the frame viewer to shorten the video.
- Tap **Done,** then tap **Save Video** to keep only the trimmed video or tap **Save Video as New Clip** to save the edited version as a different clip.

Edit Slow-Mo Videos

You can adjust a slow-motion video to play only a part of the video in slow motion. To do this,

- Open a slow-motion video and tap **Edit.**
- Pull the white vertical bars under the frame viewer to choose the video section that should be played back in slow motion.

Edit a Live Photo

You can add a filter to your Live Photo, trim the length, mute sound, or change the Key Photo.

- Open the Live Photo, tap **Edit,** and then tap ⦿.
- Drag either end of the frame viewer to trim the video.

- Tap 🔊 to mute/unmute the video.
- Tap the **Live** icon at the top of the screen to change the video to a still photo.

- To choose a key photo from the video, move the white frame on your frame viewer to the desired frame, click **Make Key Photo,** and then click **Done.**

Add Effects to Live Photos

To add effects to a Live Photo,

- Open the Live Photo and swipe up to view the effects.
- You will find three effects on your screen; tap an effect to use it on the video.
    - ✓ **Loop**: turns your Live Photo into a continuous looping video. Once the video ends, it instantly starts to play from the beginning until you stop it—best for when the subject repeats the same thing, like dancing or skipping.
    - ✓ **Long Exposure:** gives your photo a long exposure effect by blurring the motion.
    - ✓ **Bounce**: rewinds the action backward and forward until you stop it.

Edit Portrait Images

Edit Portrait photo, adjust the blur level, change, or remove lighting effects.

- Open the Portrait photo and tap **Edit.**
- Drag the ⬡ button to select a lighting effect:
    - o **Natural Light:** the subject is in sharp focus, and the background blurred.
    - o **Contour Light:** the face is decorated with dramatic shadows.

- **Studio Light:** gives the photo an overall clean look.
- **Stage Light:** gives a deep black background.
- **High-Key Light Mono:** gives a white background with a grayscale subject.
- **Stage Light Mono:** just like Stage Light, but with a black and white background.
* Use the slider under each effect to adjust the intensity of the lighting effect.

- To adjust the background blur of the image, tap ⓕ and then use the slider to adjust the effect.
- Tap **Done** to save your changes.
- Tap **Portrait** at the top of the Portrait to remove the Portrait effect.

Create an Album

Create an album to organize your images.

- Click the **Albums** tab in the Photo app, then click ➕.
- Select either **New Album** or **New Shared Album** (you can share this album with others.)
- Choose a name for the album, and then tap **Save**.
- Select the videos and photos to add to the album and then tap **Done**.

Add/ Remove Videos and Photos to an Album

To add videos and photos to an existing album,

- Go to the **Library** tab and then click on **Select**.
- Select the video and photos you want to add, then click ⬆️.
- Swipe up, click **Add to Album,** then choose an album.

To remove photos/ videos from an album,

- Open the album and then tap the video or photo.

- Tap the 🗑 button, then choose to remove the photo from the album or delete it from all your linked devices.

Edit an Album

To rearrange, rename or delete existing albums,

- Go to the Albums tab, click **See All,** and then tap **Edit.**
- To rename the album, click the album name and enter a new name.
- To delete, tap ⊖ beside the album.
- To rearrange the albums, touch and hold the thumbnail for an album, and then drag it to a different location.
- Tap **Done** to save.

Sort Photos in an Album

- Choose an album in the Album tab, tap ••• then click **Sort**.

Filter Photos in Albums

Filter videos and photos by edited, favorites, videos, and photos.

- Choose an album in the Album tab, tap ••• then click **Filter**.
- Select how you want to filter the videos and photos in the album, then tap **Done**.
- To remove a filter from the album, tap the ≡ button, tap **All Items** and tap **Done**.

Organize Albums in Folders

Add your albums to different folders to further organize the Photos app.

- Go to the Album tab, tap + and select **New Folder**.
- Enter a name for the album, then tap **Save**.
- Open the folder, tap **Edit,** and tap + to create new folders or albums inside the folder.

Revert an Edited Photo/ Video

To undo any changes you made to a video or photo and return it to the original version,

- Open the edited photo or video, and tap **Edit**.
- Tap **Revert,** then click **Revert to Original**.

Note that you would be unable to revert to the original version for a video you saved as a new clip.

Send Video Clips in Messages

You can send a video clip or picture to another person as an MMS. To do this, follow the listed steps

- Open the video or photo in the Photos app.
- Tap the share button at the left bottom side of the screen.
- On the next screen, click on **Message.**
- On the **To** field, input the receiver's details.
- Click on the **Text** area to input your message.
- Once done, click on the Send button .

Send Video Clip or Picture in an Email

Follow the steps below to attach a video or picture with your email:

- Open the video or photo in the Photos app.
- Tap the share button at the left bottom side of the screen.
- On the next screen, click on **Mail.**
- On the **To** field, input the receiver's details.
- Input your email subject on the **Subject** field.
- Click on the **Text** area to input your message.
- Once done, click on **Send** to deliver your email.

Share and Print Your Photos

To share or print,

- Open the photo and tap ⬆.
- Choose an option to share the photo – like Messages, AirDrop, or Mail.
- Swipe up and choose **Print** if you wish to print your photo.

Apply Filter to a Video

The filter tool is similar to the one you use on Instagram.

- From the photo app, choose the video you wish to edit.
- Then click on **Edit at** the top right side of your screen.

- You will see the filter menu at the bottom of the screen.
- There are nine available filters that you can navigate through for a feel on how each will look in your video.
- Pick the filter you want, and a horizontal dial will appear under the selected filter.

- Slide the dial to adjust the level of intensity of that filter.
- Once you are satisfied with the outcome, click on **Done**.

Remove Location Details from your Photos

Each time you take photos on your iPhone, the GPS records the exact location the photo was taken – this helps you view your photos based on location. This also means that people who view your pictures on their photo app can see the place you took the photo. This poses security threats, especially when sharing images on social media or to a group that you have no personal relationship with. The good news is that you can remove the location details from your photos before sharing or select persons who should view this information. Apart from photos, you can remove location details from your videos, movies, and even multiple images sent via messages, Facebook, Mail, and so on.

- To share a single video or photo, open the item, tap **Share** ⬆.

- For multiple videos and pictures, open the Album that has items, tap **Select**, then choose all the items you want before you click on the **Share** button.
- On the next screen, click on **Options.**
- Move the switch beside **Location** to the left to disable this feature.

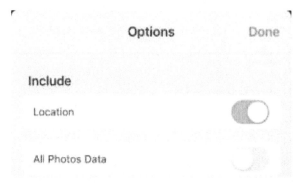

- Tap **Done.**
- Then pick the method you want to use in sending your pictures.

Note: each time you want to share a video or picture, remember to disable location, and the option is only available when sharing the photos or videos directly from your Photo app. Disabling the location feature when sharing does not remove location details from the images and videos saved on your phone.

Chapter 14: Phone App

Answer Call

Do any of the following when you have an incoming call:

- Drag the slider on the locked screen.
- Press the center button on your Earpods.
- Tap 🟢 and tap 🔴 to end the call.
- Tap the mute button to mute the call or continue to hold the mute button to place the call on hold.
- Tap **Audio** to choose an audio device for hands-free.

Call a Number

- Open the Phone app and tap **Keypads.**
- If you have a dual SIM phone and want to use a different line to call, tap the line at the top, then select a line.
- Input the number you want to call, then press the call icon—tap to clear and enter the number again.
- Tap to show the last number you dialed, then tap again to call that number.
- To paste a copied number, tap the phone number field and then select **Paste.**
- For international calls, tap and hold the "0" key until the "+" key appears.
- Tap the end call button at the bottom of the screen once done.

Redial or Return a Recent Call

- Open the Phone app and tap **Recents.**
- Then tap the number you want to call.
- Tap ⓘ to know more about the call and the caller.

Control Call Waiting

Call waiting allows you to be on a call and still get notification of another call on the same line. If call waiting is disabled, any incoming call when you are on the phone will go to Voicemail.

- From **Settings,** click on **Phone,** then click on **Call Waiting.**

- Move the switch beside **Call Waiting** to the left or right to enable or disable.

Control Call Announcement

Set the iPhone to announce your incoming calls.

- From **Settings,** go to **Phone,** then click on **Announce Call.**
- Select **Always** if you want this feature even when silent mode is enabled.
- Choose **Headphones & Car** to activate when your device is connected to a car or a headset.
- The **Headphones Only** option will be for when the device is connected to a headset.
- Select **Never** if you do not wish to turn on this feature.

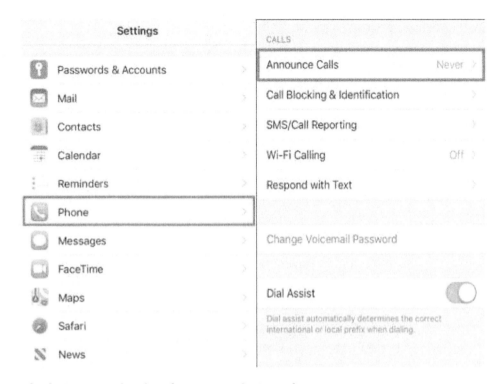

Block Communication from Certain People

Block FaceTime calls, messages, and voice calls in the Phone app.

- Open the Phone app and tap **Recents, Favorites,** or **Voicemail.**

- Tap the ⓘ button beside a contact or number you want to block, move down, and tap **Block This Caller.**

- Or tap **Contacts** in the Phone app, click a contact, move down, and tap **Block This Caller.**

Manage Your Blocked Contacts

- Tap **Phone** in the Settings app, then tap **Blocked Contacts.**
- Tap **Edit** to unblock or add more contacts.

Send Unknown Callers to Voicemail

Any calls from a number not saved on your phone will be sent to voicemail.

- Tap **Phone** in the Settings app, then tap **Silence Unknown Callers.**
- You will only receive calls from your saved numbers, recent outgoing calls & Siri suggestions.

Block Spam Callers

- Tap **Phone** in the Settings app, then tap **Call Blocking & Identification.**
- Turn on **Silence Junk Callers** to block calls from numbers that your carrier identifies as potential fraud or spam.

Make Calls using Wi-Fi

Wi-Fi Calling uses your Wi-Fi network to make and receive calls.

- Tap **Phone** in the Settings app, then tap **Cellular.**
- Choose a line under **Cellular Plans** if your iPhone has Dual SIM.
- Click on **Wi-Fi Calling,** then toggle on **Wi-Fi Calling on This iPhone.**
- Then confirm or enter an address for emergency services.

Use and Manage Call Forwarding on your iPhone

With the Call Forwarding Unconditional (CFU) feature in the iPhone, calls will go straight to a different phone number without the main device ringing. This is most useful when you do not wish to turn off the ringer or disregard a call, but you also do not want to be distracted by such calls. To enable this feature, follow the steps below:

- Tap **Phone** in the settings app and tap **Call Forwarding.**
- Select the **Forward To** option and input the second number where you want to receive the calls. It could be your voicemail.

Cancel Call Forwarding on your iPhone

- Tap **Phone** in the settings app and tap **Call Forwarding.**
- Move the slider to switch off the feature.

Manage Caller ID Settings and Call Logs on your iPhone

You can decide to hide your caller ID when calling specific numbers. Follow the steps below to activate this.

- Tap **Phone** in the settings app and turn off **Show My Caller ID.**

When you disable the feature, the called party will not see your caller ID. This is usually for security or privacy reasons.

Clear Call Logs

For every call you make on your device, there is a log saved on the phone app. To clear the call log data, follow the steps below:

- Tap **Recents** in the Phone app.
- Tap **All** and tap **Edit.**
- Tap **Clear** at the top of the screen to clear all the logs or tap beside each number to delete individual calls.
- You may also swipe left on a call, then tap **Delete.**

Chapter 15: Contacts App

Add Contacts

- Open the **Contacts** app and then tap +.
- Enter the details of your contact, including the name, phone number, address, etc.
- Once done inputting the details, tap **Done** to save.

Merge Similar Contacts

- Open the **Contacts** app on your home screen.
- Click on the contact you want to merge and click on **Edit**.
- At the bottom of the screen, click on **Link Contact**.
- Choose the other contact you want to link.
- Click on **Link** at the top right side of the screen.

Copy Contact from Social Media and Email Accounts

- Open the Settings app and click on **Accounts and Password.**
- Click on the account, e.g., Gmail.

- Toggle on **Contacts**.

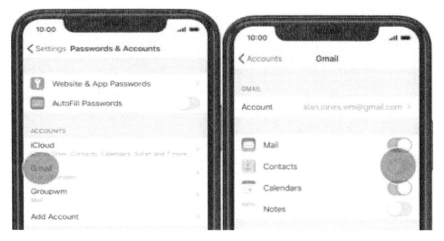

Add a Recent Caller to your Contact

- Tap **Recents** in the Phone app and tap ⓘ beside a number.
- You will see options to **Message, Call, Create New Contact, or Add to Existing Contact**.
- Select **Create New Contact**.
- Enter the caller's name and other information you have.
- At the top right hand of the screen, click on **Done**.

Save the Number you Just Dialed

- Open the Phone 📞 app and tap **Keypads**.
- Enter the phone number you want to save, then tap **Add Number**.
- Click on **Create New Contact** and enter the caller's details.
- Or click on **Add to Existing Contact**, and choose an existing contact.

- At the top right hand of the screen, click on **Done**.

Import Contacts

The iPhone allows you to import or move your contacts to your phone.

- Tap **Contacts** in the settings app and tap **Import SIM Contacts.**
- Chose the account where the contacts should be stored.
- Allow the phone to import the contacts to your preferred account or device.

Delete Contacts

Follow the steps below to delete contact

- Click on the contact you want to delete, then tap **Edit**.
- Move down and click on **Delete Contact.**
- You will see a popup next to confirm your action. Click on **Delete Contact** again.
- The deleted contact will disappear from the available Contacts.

Add Your Contact Info

Apple uses your Apple ID to create your contact card, known as My Card, but you will need to update it with your details like name and address.

- Open the Contacts app, tap **My Card** at the top of the contacts list, then click on **Edit.**
- Contacts will suggest phone numbers and addresses to set up My Card quickly.
- If you can't find **My Card,** tap ＋ and input your information.

- Then tap **Contacts** in the Settings app, tap **My Info** and click your name in the Contact list.

Create or Edit Your Medical ID

The Medical ID contains your health information that may be handle during emergencies.

- Open the Contacts app, tap **My Card** at the top of the contacts list, then click on **Edit**.
- Move down and tap **Create Medical ID** if this is your first time, or tap **Edit Medical ID** to make changes.

Turn on Do Not Disturb

Do Not Disturb silences calls and notifications, preventing them from lighting up your screen. To turn it on,

- Open the Control Center and tap 🌙 to turn on DND.
- To set the ending time, long-press the DND icon and select an option.

Even though your phone is in silent mode, you can set to receive notification from particular callers.

- Tap **Do Not Disturb** in the Settings app and then tap **Allow Calls From** to choose people that can reach you regardless of the DND.
- Turn on **Repeated Calls** to continue receiving repeated calls from the same number.

Chapter 16: Messages App

Set up iMessage

- From the Settings app, go to **Messages**.
- Enable **iMessages** by moving the slider to the right.

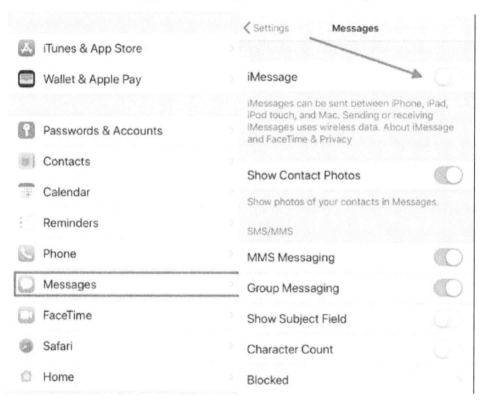

Set up Your Device for MMS

- From **Settings**, go to **Messages**.
- Enable **MMS Messaging** by moving the slider to the right.

Compose and Send Message

- Open Messages and click on an existing conversation or tap ⬜ for a new conversation.

- Enter your receiver's details in the **To** field if sending a new conversation.

- Click on the **Text Input** Field and type in your message.

- Click the send button to deliver your message.

Compose and Send Messages with Pictures/ Videos

- Open Messages and click on an existing conversation or tap for a new conversation.

- Enter your receiver's details in the **To** field if sending a new conversation.

- Click on the **Text Input Field** and type in your message.

- To insert pictures, tap , frame the shot in the viewfinder, then tap to take a new picture. To use an existing photo, tap in the app drawer, choose from your recent pictures, or tap **ALL Photos** to choose from Photos.

- To take a video, tap , swipe to Video mode, and tap .

- Then tap to send your message.

Reply to a Message

- Click on a conversation to open it and enter your message in the text field. To search for content and contacts in conversations, pull down the Messages list, and enter your search phrase in the search field.

- To replace the text with emoji, tap ⊕ or ☺, then click on each highlighted word.

- Tap ⬆ to send your message.

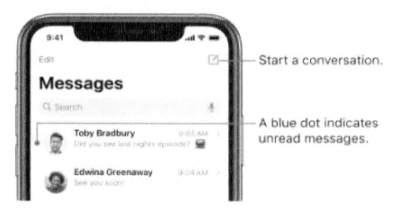

Start a conversation.

A blue dot indicates unread messages.

To respond to a specific message in a conversation (for group chats),

- Open the conversation, then touch and hold the message you want and tap ↩, enter your message and then tap ⬆.

Pin or Unpin a Conversation

Pin selected conversations to the top of the Messages list so that messages from these contacts always come first in the list.

- Tap and hold a conversation, then move it to the top of the list. Or swipe right on the conversation and then tap 📌.

- Drag the conversation to the bottom of the list to unpin or long-press the conversation, and then tap ✂.

Switch from a Conversation to an Audio Call or FaceTime

Initiate an audio call or FaceTime call with the person you are chatting with in the Messages app.

- Open a conversation and tap the name or profile picture of the contact at the top of the conversation.
- Then choose either **Audio** or **FaceTime.**

Create New Contacts from Messages On iPhone

- Go to the Messages app.
- Click on the conversation with the sender whose contact you want to add.
- Click on the sender's phone number at the top of the screen, then click on **Info** ⓘ.
- On the next screen, click on the arrow by the top right side of your screen.
- Then click **Create New Contact**.
- Input their name and other details you have on them.
- At the top right hand of the screen, click on **Done.**

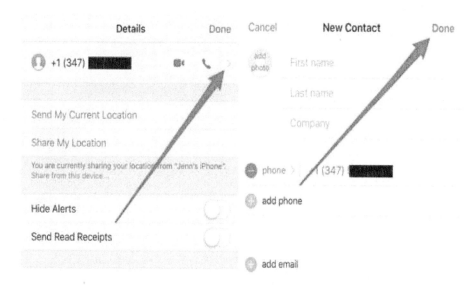

Mute Conversations

- Swipe left over a conversation you want to mute, then tap .

- A ☾ icon will appear beside the conversation, and you will no longer receive notification for that conversation.

Share Your Name and Photo

When you launch the Messages app for the first time, you will receive a prompt to choose your name and photo. You can then share the photo and name when you respond or start a new message. To edit your name and photo,

- Open the Messages app and tap ••• at the top right.
- Then click on **Edit Name and Photo.**
- Select a profile picture and type in your last and first names.

- You can either create your own Memoji to use as your profile picture or select from available Animoji.
- Tap **Done**.

Specify View for your Profile Picture and Name

You can choose who you will like to be able to view your profile picture and name. This setting is used to limit users who can access your details.

- Open the Messages app and tap ⦁⦁⦁ at the top right.
- Turn on the switch for **Name and Photo Sharing,** then select from the three options available for sharing your name and profile picture:
    - ✓ Use the **Contacts Only** option to share details with your saved contacts.
    - ✓ If you want the system to always prompt you to choose who to share with, click on the **Always Ask** option. Whenever you open a new message, you will see a pop up on your screen asking for permission to share details with the sender. To share your details, click on **Share,** or tap "**X**" to refuse.
    - ✓ Tap **Done** to save.

Customize Your Memoji and Animoji

You can create your own Memoji and Animoji through the steps below:

- Click on a conversation, tap 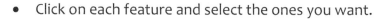, then tap ⊕.
- Click on each feature and select the ones you want.
- Tap **Done** to save the Memoji on your iPhone.

Send and Share Your Location

To share your location with a contact from Messages,

- Open a conversation with the contact, tap the name of the contact, then tap ⓘ.

- Tap **Send My Current Location** or tap **Share My Location,** then choose the duration you want.

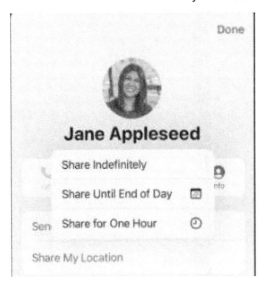

Delete a Message or Conversation

Note that you cannot retrieve deleted messages.

- To delete a single message in a conversation, long-press on the message and then tap ⬤. Tap the 🗑 button, then tap **Delete Message.**
- To delete all the messages in a conversation/ thread, tap **Delete All,** then tap **Delete Conversation.**
- You may also swipe left on an unpinned conversation, tap **Delete,** then tap **Delete** again.
- To delete multiple conversations, tap **Edit** at the top of the Messages app, tap **Select Messages,** choose the conversations you want, and tap **Delete** at the bottom.

119

To store your messages for a specified time only,

- Tap **Messages** in the Settings app, tap **Keep Messages,** then choose the period for storing the messages.

Mention People in a Conversation

When chatting in a group conversation, mention a person to call their attention to a specific person. The person might receive a notification if they configured their device to notify them.

- Open a conversation and begin typing the contact's name in the text field, then tap the name once it appears. Or type @ followed by the name of the contact.

See Mentions in Messages

To receive a notification when you are mentioned in Messages,

- Tap **Messages** in the Settings app and then tap **Notify Me.**

Change Group Name and Photo

- Tap the group number or name at the top of the conversation.
- Tap ⓘ at the upper right, choose **Change Name and Photo,** then select an option.

Send a Handwritten Message

Write your message using your finger, and the same will be sent to the receiver.

- Open a conversation and rotate to landscape orientation.
- Tap ✒ on your keyboard, write your message or select from the saved message at the bottom, then click **Done.**

- Tap to deliver the message or tap to cancel.

- Every new message you write is saved at the bottom of the handwriting screen. Click on a message to use it again. To delete saved messages, tap and hold it, then tap .

Send Money with Apple Pay in Messages

Send money to people right on the Messages app.

- Open an iMessage conversation, tap Pay and insert an amount.
- If the message contains an underlined monetary amount, click on it to set the payment amount.
- Tap **Pay** and then tap .
- Review the payment details and then authenticate the payment.

Request a Payment

Ask people to send money to you. The fund will be added to your Apple Cash card in Wallet.

- Open an iMessage conversation, tap [Pay] and insert an amount.
- Then tap **Request.**

Manage Notifications for Messages

- Tap **Notifications** in the Messages app, then tap an option to customize it. Options include:
    - Set the locations and position of message notifications,
    - Choose when to see message previews.
    - Turn on **Allow Notifications.**

Assign a Different Ringtone to a Contact

- Open Contacts and click on a contact.
- Tap **Edit,** then click on **Text Tone.**
- Choose your preference under **Alert Tones.**
- Turn on **Emergency Bypass** to allow alerts for messages received from this contact even when DND is on.

Chapter 17: Mail App

Set up Mail Account

- Tap **Passwords & Account** in the Settings app, tap **Add Account**.
- Select your email provider. Tap **Other** if the provider is not listed.

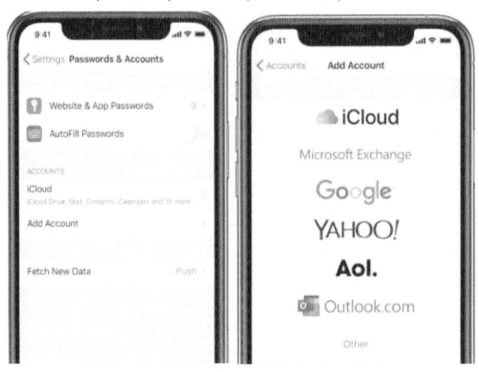

- Input your email address & password and tap **Next**.
- After the account is verified, select data from your email account, like Calendars or Contacts.
- Tap **Save** to finish.

Add Additional Mail Accounts

To add more email accounts,

- Tap **Mail** in the Settings app, tap **Account,** then tap **Add Account.**

- Tap **Other,** then tap **Add Mail Account.**
- Enter your email address, name, and password, then tap **Next.**
- Enter the names of the mail servers for your account and other requested information, then tap **Save.**

Customize Your Email Signature

The email signature will appear automatically at the end of every mail you send.

- Tap **Mail** in the Settings app, then tap **Signature.**
- Click on the text field at the upper part of your screen, then modify your signature.
- Tap **Per Account** to create different signatures for each account.

Choose a Default Email Account

When you open a new Mail, the default email address will pop-up except you choose to send with a different address.

- Tap **Mail** in the Settings app, then tap **Default Account.**
- On the next screen, click on the email address you wish to set as default.

Delete Email Account

- From Settings, go to **Accounts and Password**.
- Click on the email address you want to delete.
- Select **Delete Account** at the bottom of the page.
- On the next screen, click on **Delete from my iPhone.**

Compose and Send Email

- Open the Mail app ✉ and tap ✏.
- On the **To** field, input the receiver email address and the subject of the email.
- Write your email content in the body of the email.
- To change the formatting, tap ‹ in the format bar on top of the keyboard, then tap **Aa**. You can then change the text color and font style, add a numbered or bulleted list, and more.
- To attach a saved document, tap ‹ in the format bar on top of the keyboard, tap 📄, then select a document in the Files app. You may also drag a file to your email to attach it to the email.
- To insert a saved video or picture, tap ‹ in the format bar on top of the keyboard, tap 🖼, then click on a video or photo to insert it into your email.
- To take a video or photo, tap ‹ in the format bar on top of the keyboard, tap 📷, then take a new video or photo. Then tap **Use Video** or **Use Photo** to include it in your email.

- To scan a document into the email, tap ‹ in the format bar on top of the keyboard, tap 📷 and position your phone so that the document page shows up on your screen – your phone will automatically capture the page. To capture manually, tap the volume button or the Shutter ⊙ button. Scan as many pages as you want, then tap **Save.** You may choose to edit the document before attaching, tap ⊥ to crop, ⬤ to apply a filter, ↻ to rotate the image, or 🗑 to delete the document.
- When you finish, click on **Send** at the top right of the screen.

Reply to an Email

- Open an email, tap ↩, and then tap **Reply.**
- Enter your response and send it once done.

Quote Some Text When Replying to an Email

To quote a part of an email when sending your response,

- Open the Sender's email, long press on the first word of the text you want to quote, then drag to the last word.
- Tap ↩, tap **Reply** and then enter your response.

Always BCC Yourself

You can receive a copy of each mail you send.

- Tap **Mail** in the Settings app, then turn on **Always Bcc Myself.**

Send Email from Different Accounts

When you open a new Mail, the default email address will pop-up except you choose to send with a different address.

- Tap the **From** field to select a different account.

Block Spam and Unknown Senders

Any email received from blocked senders will be sent straight to the trash folder. Like the "silence unknown callers" feature, you are not blocking the senders as you can always go to the trash folder to see messages sent in there. At the moment, Apple has a single folder where you will see all blocked spammers and contacts. So, for all the phone numbers you may have blocked in the past either from the Messages app, FaceTime, or Phone, you can find them together with the blocked email addresses. Before this will apply to the mail app, you need to modify your block setting. This setting is what determines what the mail app should do with emails received from blocked contacts.

- Tap **Mail** in the Settings app, then go to **Threading.**
- Click on **Blocked Sender Options,** and you will see three options

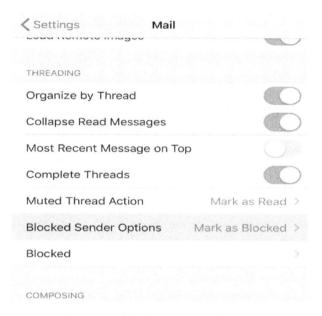

- If you enable the option for **None,** it will automatically disable the email blocking feature.
- The option, **"Mark as Blocked, Leave in Inbox,"** means that you will receive emails from your blocked contacts directly in your inbox without being notified.
- The option, **"Move to Trash,"** will send all emails from blocked contacts to the trash folder. The emails can then be deleted automatically or manually.

Note: this feature will apply to all the accounts you have in your mail app, including Outlook, Gmail, Yahoo, etc.

Block a Contact Through Their Emails

Whenever you receive an email from an unknown sender or someone you do not wish to read from again, you can get them blocked right in the mail app.

- Open an email from the sender, then tap their email address.
- Click on **Block This Contact,** then click on the prompt again to accept your action.
- And that email address is blocked!
- Every email from a blocked contact will also have a notification at the top that says, **"This message is from a sender in your blocked list,"** along with a blocked hand icon.

Unblock a Sender

For blocked email addresses, you can unblock by going to the sender's contact details in the email and then click on **"Unblock this Contact."** The hand icon may not instantly disappear, but the sender will be unblocked immediately.

Block a Contact Via Settings App

Another way to block a sender is via the settings app.

- Tap **Mail** in the Settings app, then scroll down and tap **Blocked.**
- Go to the end of the screen and click on **Add New.**
- You will receive a prompt to choose the sender to block.
- The number or email address will immediately appear on the blocked list.

Note: you need to save the contact of the person you wish to block to use this option. If you do not have the email address saved, you may have to block them from the inbox.

Unblock a Contact

- Use the steps above to access the list of blocked contacts.

- Then short swipe from the left side of the email address or phone number you want to unblock.
- After which, you click on **Unblock.**
- Alternatively, you can make a long swipe on the contact to unblock it automatically.
- Another way is to click on **Edit** at the right top of your screen, click on the /button beside the email address or phone number you want to unblock, and then click on **Unblock.**

Receive Notification of Replies

Create mail notifications when writing or reading emails.

- When drafting an email, click on the **Subject** field, tap the button, then tap **Notify Me.**
- When reading an email, tap , then click **Notify Me.**

Mute Email Notifications

To mute notifications of messages in a conversation,

- Open the email, tap , then click **Mute.**

To customize what should happen to the muted emails,

- Tap **Mail** in the Settings app, and tap **Muted Thread Action.**
- Then choose an option.

Reorder Your Mailboxes

Rearrange the mailboxes so that the ones you use frequently will come on top of the Mailboxes list.

- Tap **Mailboxes** on the top left side, then tap **Edit.**
- Long-press the ≡ icon beside a mailbox until it lifts, then move it to a different position.

Delete Emails

Use any of the options below to delete an email:

- Open an email and tap 🗑 at the end of the screen.
- Open the Mail app and swipe left on an email, then tap **Trash.**
- Swipe left all the way to the left to delete in a single gesture.
- To delete several emails, open Mails, tap **Edit,** choose the emails you want to discard, then tap **Trash.**

You will be prompted to confirm your decision to delete emails. To turn off this confirmation,

- Tap **Mail** in the Settings app, and then turn off **Ask Before Deleting.** Turn it on again if you change your mind.

Recover Deleted Emails

- Open the Trash mailbox and click on an email.
- Tap ↩, and then move the message to a different mailbox.

Archive Instead of Delete

Rather than deleting your emails, you can archive them in the Archive mailbox. This doesn't stop you from deleting unwanted emails.

- Tap **Mail** in the Settings app, and tap **Accounts.**
- Select your email account, tap **Mail,** then tap **Advanced.**

- Now change the destination mailbox for discarded emails to **Archive Mailbox.**

After you turn on this option, see below how to delete an email:

- Tap and hold the 🗑 button, then select **Trash Message.**

Decide How Long To Keep Deleted Emails

Choose how long deleted emails can stay in the Trash mailbox

- Tap **Mail** in the Settings app, and tap **Accounts.**
- Select your email account, tap **Mail,** then tap **Advanced.**
- Tap **Remove** and choose a time interval.

Note that iCloud discards every deleted email after 30 days and will override your selection even if you choose Never.

Print an Email

- Open the email, tap ↩, then tap **Print.**

Print a Picture or Attachment

- Open the email that has the attachment, open the attachment, tap ⬆, then select **Print.**

Chapter 18: Manage Applications and Data

Install Apps from the App Store

- Open the app store and click on **Search**.
- Type the name of the app into the search field and tap **Search** on your keyboard.
- Select the desired app.
- Click on **GET** beside the app and follow the steps on the screen to install the app. For paid apps, click on the price to install.

Delete Apps

To delete third-party apps installed on your phone,

- Long-press on the app until it begins to jiggle.
- Tap **Remove App**⊖, tap **Delete App,** then select **Delete.**

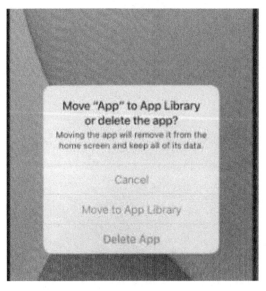

Share or Give an App

- Tap the app to view the app's details.

- Tap ⬆️ and select a sharing option or tap **Gift App** for paid apps.

Use an App Clip

App clips are a small part of an app that allows you to perform tasks on the app without downloading and installing the app. You can use the app clip for different apps and even in the real world to order food, pay for parking, or rent a bike. You can open app clips in one of the following ways:

- Tap the app link in Messages, Safari, or Maps.
- Place your iPhone close to the near-field communications (NFC) tag.

- Use your iPhone camera to scan the QR code at a physical location like a payment terminal.

The app clip card will pop-up at the bottom of the screen. To find an app clip you used recently,

- Go to the App Library and tap **Recently Added.**

Remove App Clips

To delete app clips,

- Tap **App Clips** in the Settings app, then tap **Remove All App Clips.**

Move Between Apps

Switching Apps can be tricky without a home button, but the below steps will make it as seamless as possible.

- To open the App Switcher, swipe up from the bottom of the screen and pause in the center of the screen.
- Release your finger once the app thumbnails appear.
- To flip through the open apps, swipe left or right, and tap the app you want.

Switch Between Open Apps

Here is one quick way to switch between open apps on your iPhone.

- Swipe left or right along the bottom edge of your screen.

Force Close Apps in the iPhone

You do this mostly when an app isn't responding.

- Merely swiping up from the bottom of the screen will show the app switcher. This will display all the open apps in card-like views.
- To force close the app, locate the app from the app switcher and swipe up to close the app.

Multitask with Picture-in-Picture

Picture-in-Picture allows you to watch a video or use FaceTime while performing other tasks on your iPhone.

- Tap [icon] in the video or FaceTime window to scale it down to a corner of your screen. You can then open another app.
- Pinch open to increase the size of the window, pinch closed to shrink the size.
- Tap the video window to show and hide the controls.
- To move the window, drag it to another side of your screen.
- Drag the window off the right or left end of your screen to hide it.
- Tap [icon] to close the window.
- Tap [icon] to return to the full-screen view for the app.

Delete Apps Without Losing App Data

This option will delete an app while retaining the app icon and user data.

- From the **Settings** app, click on **General**.
- Click on **iPhone Storage**.
- Click on the app you wish to uninstall and click on **Offload App**.
- Select **Offload App** again to complete.

Control Automatic App Update

- Open the **Settings** app, and click on the banner with your name and your profile picture at the top of the screen.

- Click on **iTunes and App Store.**
- Besides the **App Update** option, move the switch left or right to enable or disable the option.

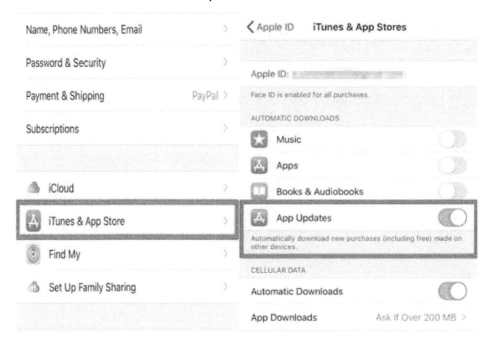

Modify Settings for Background App Refresh

When you move to a different app, some apps continue to run before they are suspended. The Background App Refresh allows suspended apps to check for new content and updates.

- From the **Settings** app, go to **General.**
- Click on **Background App Refresh.**
- To customize all your apps, click on **Background App Refresh** again and tap an option on your screen:
- To refresh the apps using Wi-fi, select **Wi-fi.**

- Select **Wi-fi and Mobile Data** if you want the system to refresh using either wi-fi or mobile data.
- Use the back button to return to the previous screen.
- Toggle on or off the button for each app to enable or disable.

Configure Your iPhone For Manual Syncing

To manually sync your data,

- Using either Wi-fi or USB, connect your iPhone to a computer.
- Manually open the iTunes app if it doesn't come up automatically.
- Tap on the iPhone icon on the top left side of the screen. If you have multiple iDevices, you will see a menu showing all the connected iDevices rather than the iPhone icon. Once the devices are displayed, select your current device.
- Tap the **Apply** button at the bottom right corner of your screen.

- Tap the **Sync** button if it doesn't start syncing automatically.

Move Apps around the Home Screen

- Long-press on an app on the Home Screen, then click **Edit Home Screen.**

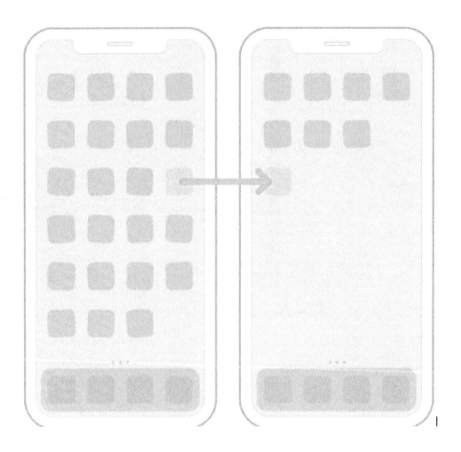

- Then drag the app to the dock at the bottom of your screen or another location on the same page. To drag the app to a different Home Screen page, drag the app to the right end of your screen and wait for the next page to appear.
- Tap **Done** to exit.

Return the Home Screen to its Original Format

Reset the home screen to discard any changes made.

- Tap **General** in the Settings app.
- Tap **Reset,** then tap **Reset Home Screen Layout.**

Open Apps on iPhone

- Swipe up from the bottom end of your screen to go to the end screen.
- Swipe through the different pages to view the apps.
- Then click on an app to open it.
- Swipe up from the bottom end of your screen to go to the first Home Screen page.

Explore the App Library

The App Library contains all your apps, sorted into categories like Entertainment, Social, and so on. You will find your frequently used apps at the top of the screen. To go to App Library,

- Swipe up to go to the Home screen, then swipe left to the end.
- Tap an app to open it.
- For app categories that have more than four apps,
- You will find a few small app icons under categories with more apps – tap the small icons to view all the apps in that category.

- To find an app, tap the search field at the top, then enter the app name to find it.
- To add an app to the Home Screen, long-press on the app, then select **Add to Home Screen.**

Add New Apps to Home Screen and App Library

Set up your iPhone to install new apps on both the **Home Screen and App Library.**

- Tap **Home Screen** in the Settings app, then choose an option.

Perform Quick Actions

Use this option to perform quick actions like Send Location, Take a Selfie, take New Notes, etc.

- Touch and hold an app until you see the Quick Actions menu.

For example,

- Tap and hold the Camera app, then choose **Record Video.**
- Tap and hold the Maps app and choose **Send My Location.**

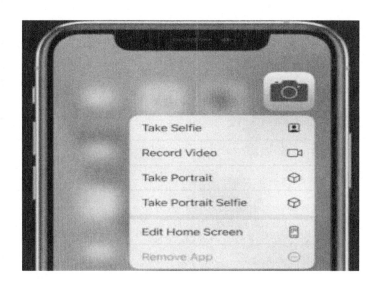

Chapter 19: The Reminders App

Create Reminders with subtasks and attachments, then mark it as complete when the task is done.

Create a Reminder

- Launch the reminders app and tap **New Reminder.**
- Enter the details for the reminder.
- Tap [calendar icon] to choose a due date for the reminder.
- Tap [location icon] to add a location to the reminder. You need to turn on location services to receive location-based notifications.
- Tap [person icon] to assign the reminder to a contact, including yourself.
- Tap [camera icon] to attach a scanned document or photo.
- Tap [flag icon] to mark an important reminder.
- Tap [info icon] to add more details to the reminder: enter more information about the reminder in the Notes field, and input a web address in the URL field.
- Tap **Priority** to choose a priority for the reminder.
- To get a reminder when chatting with a contact in Messages, toggle on **When Messages,** then pick a contact. You will see the reminder on your screen when next you message the contact.

- Tap **Done** to save the reminder.

If you did not assign a time to your reminder, the notification will pop-up by 9:00 a.m. To change the time when your all-day reminder notification appears,

- Tap **Reminders** in the Settings app, tap the time under **All-Day Reminders,** and choose a time.

Add SubTasks

You can create a subtask for every reminder.

- Open a reminder, then click the ⓘ icon at the top right side of your screen to see the available options.
- Go down on the next screen and click on **Subtasks.**
- Then click on **Add Reminder** to include a subtask.
- You can add as many subtasks as you want in a single task.
- Note that moving, completing, or deleting the parent task will also move, complete or delete the subtask.

Create a List

You can group all your tasks into a single list to make room on your reminder app's home page.

- Open the reminders app.
- Navigate to the bottom right and then click on **Add List.**

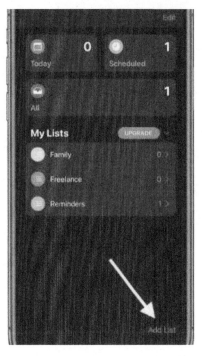

- Enter a name for your list and choose a logo and color to help you identify each list at a glance.
- Click on **Done** at the right top side of your screen.
- To add reminders or tasks to this list, click on the list under **My List**, tap the ⓘ icon, then choose the reminders that you want to add to the list.

- To add an existing task to a list, open the task, then click on the ⓘ icon at the top of your screen. Click on **List,** then click on the desired list.

Note: to quickly find a task, you can search using the search bar option.

Add a List to a Group

You can add all the lists that fall in the same category into a general group. Say you have one list for anniversaries and another for birthdays; you can have a group titled "memorable dates" and then move the lists into this group to make your home page look more appealing.

- From the Reminder app's homepage, click on **Edit** at the right top corner of your screen.
- Then click on **Add Group** at the bottom left of your screen.
- Type the name you want for the group and then select the lists that should go into that group.
- Click on **Done.**
- To modify the lists in each group, click on **Edit** again.
- Then click on the ⓘ icon.
- With the *Include* option, you can remove or add lists.

 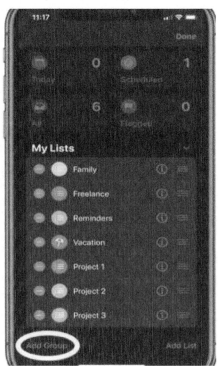

Today Notification Feature

By default, the reminders app notifies you of your tasks for the day, but you can choose not to receive any notification.

- From the settings app, click on **Reminders**.
- You can choose to turn off notifications entirely or change the timing for the notification under **Today Notification**.

Use Siri as a Reminder

Siri can do many things, which include asking the virtual assistant to remind you of a task. You can say to Siri, "remind me to," followed by the information. If you want Siri to tell you at a specific place or time, ask.

Mark Reminder as Complete

- Click the empty circle beside a reminder to mark it as complete.
- This will also hide the reminder. To unhide your completed reminders, tap ⋯ and select **Show Completed.**

Edit Multiple Reminders

- Tap ⋯, press **Select Reminders,** and click on the reminders you want to edit.
- Then use the buttons at the end of the screen to flag, assign, move, delete, complete, or add a date and date to the selected reminders.

Edit a Reminder

- To delete a reminder, swipe left on the reminder, then press **Delete.** Double-tap with three fingers to recover the deleted reminder.
- To move the reminder to a different list, click the reminder, tap ⓘ, press **List,** then select a list.

Share a List Using iCloud

Share a list with other iCloud users. Once they accept, they can then edit or mark the reminders as completed.

- Open a list, tap ⋯, and then click on **Share List.**
- Then choose how you want to send your invitation.

Chapter 20: Find My

The Find My iPhone and Find My Friends apps were collapsed into a single app called **"Find My."** This new app allows you to find your missing devices and share your location with your loved ones.

Set Up Location Sharing

Before you can share your location, you need to set up location sharing.

- Open Find My and tap **Me,** then enable **Share My Location.**
- You will find the device sharing your location under **My Location.**
- If your iPhone isn't sharing your location, scroll down, and click **Use This iPhone as My Location.**

Share Your Location

- Open the **Find My** app on your home screen.
- Navigate to the **People** tab to see your current location.
- Scroll down and tap **Share My Location.**
- Type the name of the contact you want to send your location.
- Tap **Send** and select your sharing method.

Stop Sharing Your Location

Hide your location from a friend or everyone. To hide from one person,

- Go to the People tab and click on the person you don't want to share your location with.
- Click **Stop Sharing My Location,** then select **Stop Sharing Location.**

To hide your location from everyone,

- Go to the **Me** tab and disable **Share My Location.**

Respond to a Location Sharing Request

Your friends can send a request to know your present location.

- Go to the **People** tab and click **Share** below the friend's details that sent the request, then select how long you want to share your details.
- Tap **Cancel** to decline the sharing request.

Stop Receiving Location Sharing Request

To prevent others from requesting to know your location,

- Go to the **Me** tab and disable **Allow Friend Requests.**

Add an iPhone, iPod Touch, or iPad

Before you can find a missing device, you need to add the device to Find My.

- Tap your name in the Settings app, then tap **Find My.**
- Sign in with your Apple ID if prompted, then tap **Find My (device)**

- Then turn on **Find My (device)** and enable any of the following:
    - ➢ **Send Last Location:** once your iPhone battery level goes critically low, the location is automatically sent to Apple.
    - ➢ **Find My network or Enable Offline Finding:** to find your device even when it's offline.

Find Missing Device

- Go to the tab for **Devices** to see all the registered Apple devices.
- Select the missing device, and you will see the following options on your screen: ***Mark As Lost,*** **Get Directions** to the device, **remotely** *Erase This Device,* or *Play Sound.* Select the option that bests suit your needs.
- If the device offline when this action was performed, you can choose to receive a notification once the device comes online. To do this, click the **Notify When Found** option under **Notifications.**

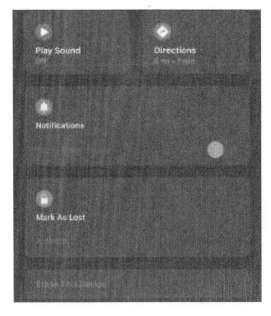

Get Direction to a Device

To get detailed direction to your iPhone's current location,

- Go to the **Devices** tab and click on the missing device.
- Tap **Directions** to launch Maps, then tap the route to begin navigation to the device's location.

Remove a Device from Find My

Remove an iPhone that you no longer use from the devices list.

- Go to the **Devices** tab and click on the device.
- Click **Remove this Device,** then select **Remove.**

Disable Activation Lock

Turn off Activation Lock on a device that is no longer in your possession or that you gave away.

- Go to the **Devices** tab and click on the device.
- Tap **Erase This Device,** then click **Erase This (device).**
- Tap **Erase,** enter your Apple ID password, and tap **Erase** again.
- For offline device, the remote erase will start when the device connects to a cellular or Wi-Fi network. You will receive an email to confirm that the device is erased.
- Once erased, tap **Remove this Device,** then click on **Remove.**
- This will erase all the content on the iPhone, and someone else can now activate the iPhone.

Chapter 21: Apple Maps

Use Your Precise Location on Maps

Turn on Precise Location for accurate directions to your destinations.

- Tap **Privacy** in the Settings app, then tap **Location Services.**
- Tap **Maps** and turn on **Precise Location.**

View Details about a Place

To see more details about a place like the business hours, phone number, customer reviews, etc.,

- Enter the address or location in the search bar, then tap the place on the map.
- Tap **Directions** to get a route to the place.
- Swipe up on the information card to view details about the location.
- Tap ✕ to exit.

Share Places in Maps

To share a place or location with others,

- Tap the location on the map, tap ⬆ and select an option.

Add a Place to your Favorites

- Open Maps and pull up the top of the search to display Favorite.
- Tap ✚ under **Favorites,** then select a suggestion below the search field or enter an address in the search field and click on the result.

- Tap the title to rename the favorite, then set a new name.
- Tap **Done** to save the place.

Here is another way to add a location to Favorites,

- Tap the location on the map and tap **Add to Favorites** at the bottom of the information card.
- Swipe up from the top of the search card to view your favorites.
- Tap **See All** to view all the Favorites, then swipe left on an item to remove it from Favorites.

Use the Look Around Feature in Apple Maps

If you are familiar with the Streetview from Google, you can relate to Apple's Look Around Feature. This feature allows you to preview a particular location before you physically visit. The steps below will guide you on use this feature.

- Type your desired location in the Apple Map's search bar.
- Then press long on the map to select this location.
- You will find the 🔭 icon on locations that supports the **Look Around** feature.
- Click on the **Look Around** 🔭 image to go to the street level and then drag to look around the location.
- This screen also shows you facts about the location, and you can swipe up from the bottom of your screen to add the area to your favorites list.
- Tap elsewhere on the map to view a different point of interest.

- Pinch closed or open to zoom out or in.
- Tap ⬈ or ⬊ to switch from or to full-screen view.
- To hide labels in a full-screen view, click the information card at the end of the screen and then tap .
- Tap **Done** to exit.

Explore New Places with Guides

Guides help you discover great places all over the world –places to shop, eat, and explore.

- Click on the search field in the Map app, then use any of the options below to open a Guide:
    - Swipe down, select a publisher, and click a cover.
    - Tap **See All,** choose an option at the top, then click on a cover.
    - Click on a cover under **Editors' Picks**
- Tap ⬇ to save the guides to your collection.
- Tap ⬆ to share it.
- Tap ➕ to add a destination in the guides to your Guides collection.
- Tap ❌ to go to the search field.

Choose Your Preferred Type of Travel

Set your default mode of transportation in Maps.

- Tap **Maps** in the Settings app and choose your preference under **Prefered Type of Travel.**

Get Driving Directions

- Enter a destination in Maps, click on the destination, then tap **Directions.**
- Tap the 🚗 icon for driving, then tap **Go** beside a route.
- Alternatively, enter a destination in Maps, touch and hold the spot on the map, tap **Directions, and** then tap the 🚗 icon.

- As you move, Maps speaks turn-by-turn directions leading to your destination.
- Tap **End** to complete the trip or say something like, "Hey Siri, stop the navigation."

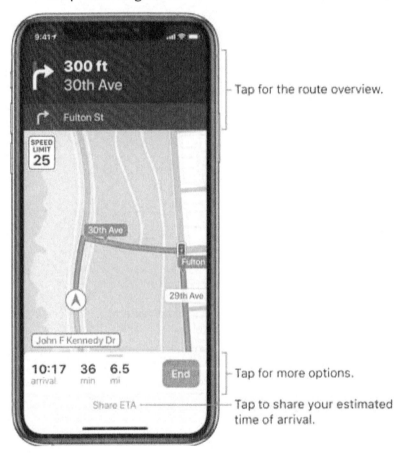

Get Cycling Directions from Your Current Location

Receive detailed cycling directions in Maps, covering routes on bike lanes, bike-friendly roads, and bike paths. As you move, Maps speaks cycling-specific directions for maneuvers and turns.

- Enter a destination in Maps, click on the destination, then tap **Directions**.

- Tap the 🚲 icon for cycling, then tap **Go** beside a route you want.

- Alternatively, enter a destination in Maps, touch and hold the spot on the map, tap **Directions, and** then tap the 🚲 icon.

Turn Off Voice Directions

To mute the voice directions or adjust the volume,

- Tap **Maps** in the Settings app, tap **Navigation & Guidance** and select an option under **Navigation Voice Volume.**

Chapter 22: Safari

Safari is the default browser available on all Apple devices, including the iPhone.

Access Website Settings for Safari

Similar to how it works on the Safari browser for Mac, you can modify security and viewing options for different websites. Safari then applies the settings so that you do not have to run them repeatedly. The steps below will show you how to achieve this.

- Visit a site that you use regularly.
- Tap on the AA icon at the left top corner of your screen to show the **View menu** option of the website.
- Tap the Large A or small A to increase or decrease the font size.
- Tap **Hide Toolbar** to hide the search field for that webpage. Tap the top of the screen to return the search field.
- Click on **Show Reader View** to remove navigation or ads menus on the webpage.
- Select **Request Desktop Website** for the desktop version of that webpage.
- Tap **Website Settings** to set privacy and display controls for all the times you visit this website.

Access Safari Download Manager

The download manager shows you a list of items that are downloading and ones that were downloaded previously. When you attempt to download a file, a little download icon will appear at the right top corner of your screen. When you click on this icon, you will see how far the download has gone. Click on the magnifying glass beside the downloaded file to go straight to the folder where the file is stored, whether in the cloud or on your phone's local storage.

Auto-Close Open Tabs in Safari

For several users, when you launch the Safari browser, you will find several open tabs from social media posts to Quora to Google searches. For most of these opened tabs, you may not go back to them, but it could be quite bothersome to close each tab individually. The good news is that there is now a feature that can automatically close open tabs in the Safari browser after a defined time. The steps below will show you how to manage the option.

- From the settings app, click on **Safari.**
- Click on **Tabs** then click on **Close Tabs.**
- The next screen will show a timeline for open tabs to close. The default option is "**Manually.**"

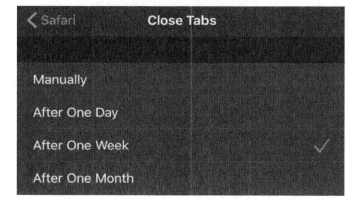

- You can pick from the other options if you desire: **After One Week, After One Day** or **After One Month.**

Modify Where Downloaded Files from Safari are Saved

By default, all downloaded files are saved in the **Download folder** of the Files app, but you can modify this by selecting an alternative storage location with the steps below:

- Tap **Safari** in the Settings app and click on **Downloads.**

 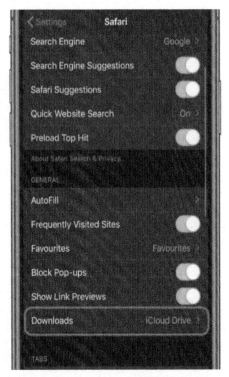

- You can then make your choice from the available options: On My iPhone, iCloud Drive, or in another location that you want.

Choose When Downloaded File List is Cleared

By default, the downloaded file list clears at the end of each day. You can change this setting to manually clear the list or clear the list once the download is complete.

- From the Settings app, click on **Safari.**
- Click on **Downloads** and select **Remove Download List Items**.
- Make your pick from the three available options on your screen: **Upon successful download, After one day,** or **Manually.**

 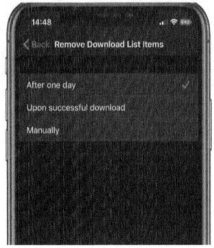

Enable Content Blockers in Safari

Content blockers help to prevent ads like banners and popups from loading on a website you visit. They also disable cookies, scripts, and beacons that sites attempt to load, which in turn protects your privacy from online tracking. You will need to download at least one third part content blocker to use this option.

- Tap **Safari** in the Settings app, then click on **Content Blockers**.
- To enable this option, move the switch beside it to the right.

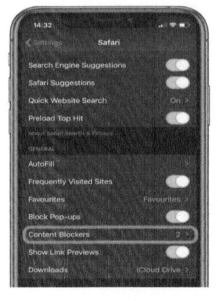

Temporarily Disable Content Blockers in Safari

Some sites require you to disable content blockers before you can access them. For sites like this, you can temporarily disable the content blocker.

- Open a website on the Safari app, then tap the AA icon at the left top corner of your screen.

- Then click on **Turn Off Content Blockers**.
- To disable this feature for just one website, click on **Website Settings** and then move the switch beside **Use Content Blockers** to the left to disable it.

Block Pop-Ups

- Tap **Safari** in the Settings app, then turn on **Block Pop-ups**.

Share or Save a Safari Web Page as a PDF

You can save a webpage as a PDF document with the steps below:

- Open a website on the Safari app, then press both the Side and the Volume Up buttons at the same time to take a screenshot.
- A preview of the screenshot will show at the left lower side of the screen.
- When you click on the preview, it will open the **Instant Markup Interface**. You need to be fast with this as you have only 5 secs before this screen disappears.

- Click on **Full-Page** in the right upper corner of the Markup interface.
- Then click on **Done** and select **Save PDF to Files** to save as PDF.
- Click on the **Share** button to share the PDF and choose who and how you want to share it.

Translate a Webpage

Translate a webpage from one language to another.

- Click AA at the top of the page, then select .

Open Link in New Tab

- To open a link in a new tab, tap and hold the link, then select **Open in New Tab.** Or tap the link with two fingers.

To remain on the current tab when you launch a link in a new tab,

- Tap **Safari** in the Settings app, tap **Open Links,** then select **In Background.**

Bookmark a Webpage

Bookmark webpages that you want to visit later. The webpages are saved in your Bookmark folder for easy and fast view.

- Open a website, tap and hold , then click **Add Bookmark.**

Add Webpage to Favorites

Add your frequently visited sites to Favorite, and you will see the websites whenever you launch Safari.

- Open a website, tap , then click **Add to Favorites.**

- To edit the favorites, tap 📖, click the Bookmarks tab, click **Favorites,** then click Edit to rename, rearrange or delete your favorites.

Add Website Icon to your Home Screen

Add a website icon to your home screen to quickly access the site.

- Open a website, tap ⬆️, then click **Add to Home Screen.**

Browse Open Tabs

- Open Safari and tap 🗂️ to see all your open tabs.
- Swipe left on a tab to close it or click on the tab to open it.
- Tap and hold ⟨ or ⟩ to view a tab's history.

View Open Tabs on Other Apple Devices

To view your open tabs across all your Apple devices, you need to sign in with your Apple ID on all the devices, then follow the steps below:

- Tap your name in the Settings app, tap **iCloud,** then turn on **Safari**
- Open Safari, tap 🗂️ and then scroll to the bottom to see the open tabs on your other devices. Swipe left to close a tab.

Chapter 23: Gaming

You can now take your gaming experience to the next level by playing games on your iPhone with the DualShock 4 or the Xbox One Controller. The **Xbox One** controller has to be 100% charged.

Pair your iPhone with an Xbox One controller

- Tap **Bluetooth** in the settings app, then turn on **Bluetooth.**
- Press the Xbox logo button to power it on.
- Go to the back of the controller and press the wireless enrollment button there. Hold down the button for some seconds.
- Please skip this step if you have already unpaired the controller from a different device. You can press and hold the Xbox button to put it in pairing mode.
- If you haven't unpaired before, continue with the steps below.
- The Xbox button light will begin to flash quickly.
- Go to your Bluetooth menu on your smartphone and locate the **"Xbox Wireless Controller"** from the list, then click on it.
- Once the light stops blinking and remains focused, then you know that pairing is complete.

Pair your iPhone with a DualShock 4

- Tap **Bluetooth** in the settings app, then turn on **Bluetooth.**
- Press both the Share and PlayStation Button of the controller simultaneously and hold down for a few seconds.

- You should see lights begin to flash intermittently at the back of the controller.
- Go to the Bluetooth menu on your iPhone, and you will find the **DualShock 4 Wireless controller** as one of the devices on the displayed list. Click on the controller.
- Once the blinking light at the back of the controller changes to a reddish-pink color, it means that the devices have paired.

Unpair Game Controller from your iPhone

To unpair a game controller from your device,

- Tap **Bluetooth** in the Settings app.
- Tap the ⓘ button beside a controller, then tap **Forget This Device**.
- Repeat the steps above to pair it with your iPhone.

Chapter 24: Screenshots

Take a Screenshot

- Press both the side and the Volume Up buttons simultaneously to take a screenshot.
- Then click on the little preview in the lower-left corner of your screen and tap **Done**.
- You will find a pop-up to either save the image or delete the screenshot.
- Click on **Save to Files** to save the screenshots in the Files app or your preferred location other than the Photos app.

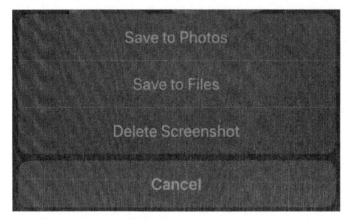

- If you selected **Save to Photos,** open the Photos app to view all your screenshots in the Screenshot album or the **All Photos** album if you turned on iCloud Photos in the Settings app.
- To quickly get a PDF of an email, document, or webpage, take a screenshot, tap the thumbnail at the bottom left, then select **Full Page**.

Scan a Document

- Open the Notes app and click on an existing note or tap ⌁ to create a new one.

- Tap the 📷 button, then select **Scan Documents**.

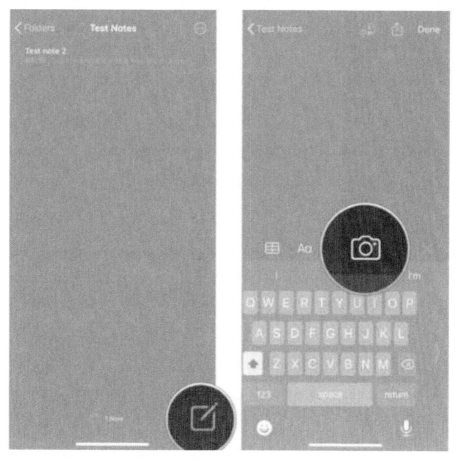

- Arrange the documents you want to scan in front of your phone camera, and the document will automatically scan if your device is in Auto mode. If the scanner doesn't automatically scan the documents, tap any of the Volume buttons or the Shutter button.

- Drag the corners of the scanned file to fit the page, then click **Keep Scan.**
- Tap **Save** when you finish scanning all the documents.

Sign a Document

- Open the document in the Notes app, then tap the button.
- Tap **Markup** , tap the button, then tap **Signature.**
- Select from your saved signatures or create a new signature, then adjust the signature box's size and move it to any part of the document. Tap **Done** to finish.
- To manually sign your document, tap **Markup** on the document, choose a tool on your screen, then sign the document with your finger. Tap **Done** to save.

Create a Screen Recording

Create a recording of your screen and include sound on your recording.

- Tap **Control Center** in the Settings app and tap beside **Screen Recording.**
- Open the Control Center, press and wait for three seconds.
- To stop recording, go to the Control Center, tap the red status bar or the button at the top of your screen, then tap **Stop.**

Chapter 25: Wifi and Connectivity

Join a Wi-fi Network

- Go to **Settings**, then click on **Wi-Fi.**
- Move the switch beside **Wi-fi** to the right to put on the Wi-fi.
- Select your Wi-fi network from the drop-down.
- Type in the password and click on **Join.**

Control Wi-fi Setup

- From the top right side of the screen, draw down the screen.
- Click on the Wi-fi icon to enable or disable.
- Move the switch beside **Wi-fi** to the right or left to put off or on.

Control Mobile Data

- Go to **Mobile Data** under **Settings.**
- Move the switch beside **Mobile Data** to the right or left to put off or on.
- Scroll to where you have the applications and move the switch beside each app to the right or left to put off or on.

Control Automatic Use of Mobile Data

- Go to **Mobile Data** under **Settings.**
- Move the switch beside **Wi-fi Assist** to the right or left to put off or on.

Control Data Roaming

- Go to **Mobile Data** under **Settings.**
- Click on **Mobile Data Options.**

- Move the switch beside **Data Roaming** to the right or left to put off or on.

Use Your iPhone as a Hotspot

- Go to **Personal Hotspot** under **Settings**.
- Move the switch beside **Personal Hotspot** to the right or left to put off or on.
- IF wi-fi is disabled, click **Turn on Wi-fi and Bluetooth.**
- Select **Wi-fi and USB only** if wi-fi is enabled already.
- Input the wi-fi password beside the field for a wi-fi password.
- Select **Done** at the top of the screen.

Download Large Apps over Cellular Network

When downloading apps above 200MB, you will see a popup to confirm if you want to continue the download using cellular data, or you will download it "**Later on Wi-Fi.**" But you have to enable this feature first.

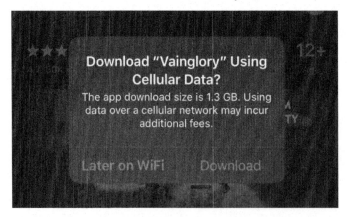

- From the settings app, click on **iTunes & App Store.**
- On the next screen, click on the appropriate option.

✓ **Always Allow** will complete your download without any further confirmation.

✓ **Ask If Over 200MB** if you want to choose either Wi-fi or cellular.

✓ **Ask First** will require your confirmation before any download over 200MB.

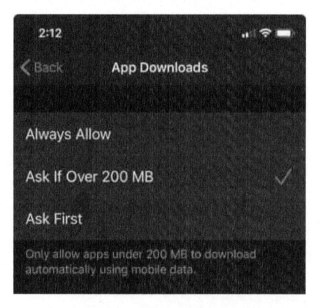

Chapter 26: Battery Tips

The iPhone battery tends to run down fast because of the different functions that the iPhone offer. I have compiled a list of things you can do to save your battery life.

Set Optimized Battery Charging

Optimized Battery Charging reduces wear on your phone battery and improves the battery lifespan by reducing the time your smartphone spends fully charged. With this feature enabled, your device will stop charging past 80% in most cases. The processor is designed to activate this feature only when it predicts that the phone will stay connected to a charger for a long time.

- From the Settings app on your smartphone, click on **Battery.**
- Click **Battery Health** and turn on **Optimized Battery Charging.**

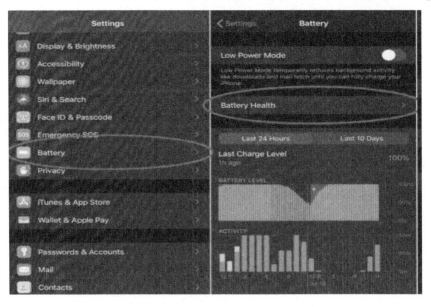

Disable Auto Update of Apps

You may have set up the option to update your apps automatically as soon as there is a new version, which can drain the battery life. Follow the steps below to disable this feature and manually update your apps.

- Tap your name in the Settings app, then tap **iTunes & App Store**.

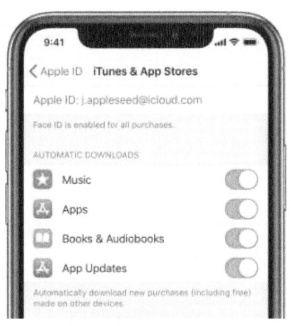

- Then turn off **App Updates**.

Stop Background Apps Refresh

One feature built to make your iPhone not only smart but also ready for use when needed is the Background App Refresh. The feature looks out for apps that you use often and the period in the day that you use these apps and then carry out automatic updates on the app to give you the latest information the next time you launch the app. This setting is great, but battery consuming. Turn it off when low on battery.

- Go to the settings app and click on **General.**
- Then click on **Background App Refresh**.
- Move the slider to the left to disable this feature for all your apps or select apps.

Extend the Device Battery Life

Some apps and services on the iPhone draw lots of power, which will drain the battery life faster. You can turn on low power mode to reduce power consumption by disabling automatic downloads, background app refresh, mail fetch, and some visual effects – this can give you another three hours.

- From **Settings**, go to **Battery**.
- Move the switch beside **Low Power Mode** to the right to enable.

Reduce Screen Brightness

The brighter your screen is, the more power it consumes. You can control your phone's brightness using the slider on your iPhone. When you need to save battery, ensure that the brightness of the screen is at its lowest.

- From the settings app, click on **Display & Brightness**
- Then use the slider to reduce the brightness by pulling to the left.

Disable Auto App Suggestions

This feature uses your location service to discover your area and suggest apps that you may need based on your location. While it is a cool feature, it can, however, drain the battery. To disable

- Open the Settings app and click on **Siri & Search.**

- Under **Siri Suggestion,** toggle off **Suggestions in Search** and **Suggestions in Look Up.**
- You may also toggle off **Suggestions on Lock Screen.**

Stop Motion and Animations

This setting will reduce the sliding, panning, and zooming visible on your iPhone screen and when using apps.

- From the settings app, click on **General,** then tap **Accessibility.**
- Select **Reduce Motion,** then move the slider beside **Reduce Motion** to the right to turn it on.

Disable Wi-Fi When Not in Use

When not using the Wi-Fi connection, it is advisable to disable it so it does not drain your battery.

- From the settings app, click on **Wi-Fi.**

- Then move the slider beside **Wi-Fi** to disable it.

Disable Bluetooth

Bluetooth is another function that transmits data wirelessly and drains battery while doing so. To save your battery life, then I will advise that you put on Bluetooth only when needed. To either disable or enable your device Bluetooth, go to settings, and click on **Bluetooth.**

Locate the Battery Draining Apps

You can find apps using a significant percentage of your battery through a feature called **Battery Usage.** Follow the steps below to use this step

- From the Settings app, click on **Battery.**
- Select the view details for the last ten days or the last 24 hours.
- Scroll down to see how each app used the battery.

Ensure that Personal Hotspot is Disabled

When the hotspot is on, your iPhone becomes a hotspot that shares its cellular data with other devices in range. While it can be useful, it can also drain your battery. Turn it off when not in use.

- Go to the Settings app, tap **Personal Hotspot,** and turn it off.

Disable Location Services

The iPhone comes with a built-in GPS, which is quite helpful for locating nearby restaurants, stores, etc. and finding directions. This app needs to send data over a network that usually tells on the battery of your device. Whenever you are not making use of the location services, you can disable it with the steps below:

- Go to the Settings app, tap **Privacy** & tap **Location Services.**

- Toggle off **Location Services**, then click **Turn Off** to disable the option.
- Alternatively, you can scroll down to select apps that should not access location services.

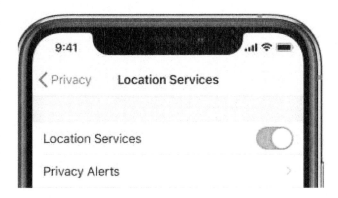

Disable Cellular Data

Like Bluetooth, when using 4G, 5G, LTE, and other cellular connections with fast transfer speeds, they tend to drain your phone battery. They even consume more power when using it heavily, like when making HD calls or streaming videos. To disable it,

- From the settings app, click on **Cellular.**
- Go to **Cellular Data** and move the switch to the left to disable.

Note: Turning off cellular data will not affect your Wi-Fi connection.

Disable Data Push

You may have configured the email settings to automatically download messages to your smartphone as soon as they get to the email server. It is crucial to be current on your email folder; however, it can drain your battery faster when you continuously download like this. Rather than the automatic update, you can go to the Mail app and manually refresh the app to receive new messages. The steps below will show you how to disable the data push feature:

- From the settings app, click on **Passwords & Accounts.**
- Or go to **Mails** from the settings app and click on **Accounts.**
- Then click on **Fetch New Data.**
- Go to **Push** and move the switch to the left to disable.

Set Emails to Download on Schedule

If you do not want to refresh your email manually, you can schedule the emails to download at a specified time. This is a balance between the steps above – while you will not have to manually refresh the mail app, you will also not get an instant update. This method will still help to achieve the end goal, which is to save battery life.

- From the Settings app, click on **Passwords & Accounts.**
- Then click on **Fetch New Data.**
- Navigate to the bottom and choose your options. The longer the time between checks, the longer your battery life is preserved.

Set up the Screen to Auto-Lock Sooner

Auto-locking your screen helps to save your battery life. As long as your phone has something it is displaying, it will be taking out of the battery life.

- From the settings app, click on **Display & Brightness.**
- Then click on **Auto-Lock.**
- Select any of the options from 30 seconds to 5 minutes.

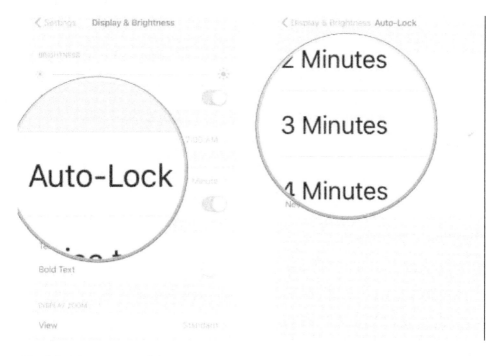

Disable Fitness Tracking

The fitness tracking feature on the iPhone is used to track your steps and other fitness activities. It is very beneficial, especially when you are trying to get into shape, but this app also drains the battery. You can disable the feature whenever you are not using it.

- From the settings app, click **Privacy** and select **Motion & Fitness**.
- Move the switch beside **Fitness Tracking** to the left to disable this feature.

Disable AirDrop When Not in Use

AirDrop is the wireless file sharing feature of the Apple devices. To use Airdrop, you need to enable both Bluetooth and Wi-Fi and prepare your phone to locate other airdrop enabled devices. This makes use of more battery, and it is advisable to disable when not in use.

- Go to the control center, then click on **AirDrop**.
- Click on **Receiving Off** to disable the feature.
- You can also go to the settings app, click on **General,** select **AirDrop** and change **Receiving Off** or **Contacts Only**.

Disable Automatic Upload of Photos to iCloud

The photo app is set to upload your photos to your device's iCloud account automatically. Disable the auto-uploads and attempt to upload only when you have a full battery or moving from your computer. Follow the steps below to check if your photos are always uploaded to iCloud.

- Go to the Settings app, tap **Photos,** then click on **iCloud Photos**

Stop Sending Diagnostic Data to Developers or Apple

The diagnostic data tell the developer how your smartphone is performing to help them produce better products. You have the option to enable this feature when setting up your device. Whenever you need to save battery life, follow the steps below to disable this option.

- Go to the Settings app, and click on **Privacy.**
- Then go to **Analytics** and shift the slider to the left to disable this feature.

Disable Vibrations

When you place your device on vibration, the phone vibrates at every notification that comes into the device. The whole process involved in this causes the battery life to go low. Follow the steps below to turn off vibrations:

- Go to the Settings app, and click on **Sounds & Haptics**
- Then move the slider beside **Vibrate on Ring** to the left to disable.

Other Helpful Tips to Improve the Longevity of Your iPhone Battery

Several factors can reduce your battery's life, like leaving your phone plugged in even after the battery is fully charged. I have compiled the list below to help you prolong your battery life.

- Do not wait for your battery to drain before charging it. Do not let the phone battery drop to below 20% before you charge.
- Do not expose the smartphone to excess heat. Avoid charging your device in a scorching environment.
- If, for any reason, you do not intend to use your phone for about a week and above, ensure that the battery drops to 80% but not below 30 percent before you power off the iPhone.
- Moving your phone quickly from a very hot to a very cold condition can affect the battery's health.
- You do not need to always fully charge your phone, as it can damage your battery.

Chapter 27: Troubleshooting the iPhone 12

This section will look at every possible challenge you may have with the iPhone and the solutions.

Most issues you experience on your iPhone can be resolved by restarting the device or doing a soft reset. If the soft reset fails to solve the problem, you can carry out other resets like the hard reset.

Restart/ Soft Reset iPhone

This is by far the most prevalent solution to most problems you may encounter on the iPhone. It helps to remove minor glitches that affect apps or iOS as well as gives your device a new start. This option doesn't delete any data from your phone; you will have your contents intact once the phone comes up.

Method 1:
- Hold both the side and Volume Down (or Volume Up) keys simultaneously until the slider comes up on the screen.
- Move the slider to the right for the phone to shut down.
- Press the **Side** button until the Apple logo shows on the screen.
- Your iPhone will reboot.

Method 2:
- Go to **Settings,** tap **General,** then click on **Shut Down.**
- This will automatically shut down the device.
- Wait for some seconds, then Hold the **Side** button to start the phone.

Hard Reset/ Force Restart an iPhone

There are some cases when you need to force-restart your phone. These are mostly when the screen is frozen and can't be turned off, or the screen is unresponsive. Just like the soft reset, this will not wipe the data on your device. It is important to confirm that the battery isn't the cause of the issue before you begin to fore-restart.

Follow the steps below to force-restart:

- Press the **Volume Up** and quickly release.
- Press the **Volume Down** and quickly release.
- Hold down the Side button until the screen goes blank and then release the button and allow the phone to come on.

Factory Reset your iPhone (Master Reset)

A factory reset will erase every data stored on your iPhone and return the device to its original form from the stores – every single data from settings to personal data saved on the phone will be deleted. You should create a backup before you go through this process. You can either backup to iCloud or iTunes. Once you have successfully backed up your data, please follow the steps below to wipe your phone.

- Tap **General** in the Settings app, then tap **Reset.**
- Chose the option to **Erase All Content and Settings**.
- When asked, enter your passcode to proceed.
- Click **Erase iPhone** to approve the action.

Depending on the volume of data on your phone, it may take some time for the reset to finish.

Once the reset is done, you may choose to set up with the **iOS Setup Assistant/Wizard,** where you can choose to restore data from a previous iOS or proceed to set the device as a fresh one.

Back-Up iPhone Using iCloud

Before you perform a factory reset, follow the steps below to back up your iPhone.

- Tap your name in the Settings app, then click **iCloud.**
- Click **iCloud Backup,** and turn on **iCloud Backup.**
- iCloud will automatically back up your device whenever it is locked, connected to power, or on Wi-Fi.
- Tap **Back Up Now** to manually back up your device.

To view your iCloud backups,

- Tap your name in the Settings app, then click **iCloud.**
- Tap **Manage Storage,** and click on **Backup.**
- To delete a backup, click on the backup, and tap **Delete Backup.**

Back-Up Using Mac

To back up on your Apple Mac,

- Use the lightning cable or USB to connect your device to the computer.
- Select your iPhone in the Finder sidebar on your Mac.
- Tap **General** at the top of the Finder window, then choose **"Back up all of the data on your iPhone to this Mac."**
- Select **Encrypt Local Bacup** to enter a password for your backup.

- Tap **Back Up Now** to complete.

Back-Up Using Windows PC

- Use a USB to connect your device to the computer, then open the iTunes app on your computer.
- Tap the iPhone button close to the upper left side of the iTunes window, then tap **Summary.**
- Scroll to **Backups** and tap **Back Up Now.**
- Select **Encrypt Local Bacup** to enter a password for your backup, enter your desired password, then tap **Set Password.**

To view your backups,

- Tap **Edit** and select **Preferences,** then tap **Devices.**

Restore iCloud Backup

After erasing your iPhone, follow the steps below to restore your iCloud backups.

- Power on your iPhone, then choose a language and region.
- Tap **Set Up Manually,** then tap **Restore from iCloud Backup** and proceed with the onscreen instructions.

Restore a Computer Backup

- Connect your iPhone to the computer that has the backup.
- Select your iPhone in the Finder sidebar on your Mac, then tap **Trust.** If using a Windows PC, click the device icon close to the upper left of the iTunes window, then tap your iPhone.
- Tap **Restore from this Backup,** select the backup, and tap **Continue.**

Chapter 28: Conclusion

With all the teachings in this book, I am confident that you will enjoy to the fullest all the fantastic features of the iPhone. The iPhone is not only a phone for making and receiving calls. With the right knowledge of using the iPhone, you can turn it into your office and achieve greater things with this device.

If you are pleased with this book's content, don't forget to recommend it to a friend.

Thank you.